D0061369

The Superpowers
and the
Syrian-Israeli
Conflict

THE WASHINGTON PAPERS

. . . intended to meet the need for an authoritative, yet prompt, public appraisal of the major developments in world affairs.

President, CSIS; David M. Abshire

Series Editor: Walter Laqueur

Director of Publications: Nancy B. Eddy

Managing Editor: Donna R. Spitler

MANUSCRIPT SUBMISSION

The Washington Papers and Praeger Publishers welcome inquiries concerning manuscript submissions. Please include with your inquiry a curriculum vitae, synposis, table of contents, and estimated manuscript length. Manuscripts must be between 120–200 double-spaced typed pages. All submissions will be peer reviewed. Submissions to *The Washington Papers* should be sent to *The Washington Papers*; The Center for Strategic and International Studies; 1800 K Street NW; Suite 400; Washington, DC 20006. Book proposals should be sent to Praeger Publishers; One Madison Avenue; New York NY 10010.

DS
119.
:S95
C63 1991

The Superpowers and the Syrian-Israeli Conflict

Beyond Crisis Management?

Helena Cobban

Foreword by Robert G. Neumann

Published with The Center for
Strategic and International Studies
Washington, D.C.

PRAEGER

New York
Westport, Connecticut
London

Library of Congress Cataloging-in-Publication Data

Cobban, Helena.
   The superpowers and the Syrian-Israeli conflict : beyond crisis
management? / Helena Cobban ; foreword by Robert G. Neumann.
      p.   cm. — (The Washington papers, ISSN 0278-937X ; 149)
   "Published with the Center for Strategic and International
Studies, Washington, D.C."
   Includes index.
   ISBN 0-275-93944-8 (alk. paper). — ISBN 0-275-93945-6 (pbk. :
alk. paper)
   1. Israel—Military relations—Syria.   2. Syria—Military
relations—Israel.   3. Israel—Military policy.   4. Middle East—
Politics and government—1979-   5. Jewish-Arab relations—1973-
I. Title.   II. Series.
DS119.8.S95C63   1991   90-25866
327.569105694—dc20

The *Washington Papers* are written under the auspices of The Center
for Strategic and International Studies (CSIS) and published
with CSIS by Praeger Publishers. The views expressed in these papers
are those of the authors and not necessarily those of the Center.

British Library Cataloging-in-Publication data is available.

Copyright © 1991 by The Center for Strategic and
International Studies

All rights reserved. No portion of this book may be
reproduced, by any process or technique, without the
express written consent of the publisher.

Library of Congress Catalog Card Number: 90-25866
ISBN: 0-275-93944-8 (cloth)
          0-275-93945-6 (paper)

First published in 1991

Praeger Publishers, One Madison Avenue, New York, NY 10010
An imprint of Greenwood Publishing Group, Inc.

Printed in the United States of America

The paper used in this book complies with the Permanent
Paper Standard issued by the National Information Standards
Organization (Z39.48-1984).

10   9   8   7   6   5   4   3   2   1

Contents

Foreword

Although the easing of superpower hostility and rivalry has becalmed, though not yet stabilized, most areas of the world, the Middle East remains the world's most explosive region. The Persian Gulf conflict is the latest example. Even this problem, far as it may be from Israel, is connected to the issue at the heart of the situation—that is, the unending Palestinian-Israeli conflict with its deep emotional impact on the entire area. Iraqi President Saddam Hussein's effort to mint the Palestinian issue has again demonstrated that this problem simply will not go away.

It is, or should be, clear to anyone that peace can be negotiated only between the adversaries—that is, the Palestinians (which, for all practical purposes, means the Palestine Liberation Organization or PLO) and the Israelis. As Professor Joseph Alpher, deputy director of the Jaffee Center of Tel Aviv University, wrote: "The PLO is the enemy; terrorism is the way it fights us [Israel]; a solution will be impossible unless we talk to it." (*Jerusalem Post*, supplement, July 7, 1990.) Yet the Palestinians and especially the PLO have now discredited themselves in the eyes of Israel and the United States by their pro-Iraq stance.

If peace can be negotiated by Israel only with the Palestinians, security for Israel can come only from the Arab states, which, in contrast to the Palestinians, have the military means of attacking Israel. Except for Egypt, however, no Arab state would normally negotiate with Israel until the Palestinian aspirations are satisfied or at least are moving in that direction. The two sets of negotiations are therefore linked, with the Palestinian-Israeli one occupying a clear priority in time. In the constantly changing kaleidoscope of the Middle East, however, Syria has now emerged as a possible candidate for participation in peace talks.

The Arab states are not united, nor do they take similar positions on the issue of peace with Israel. They will certainly not act without Palestinian support. And the most influential of the Arab states — Syria — in turn is strongly influenced by its relations with and support from the Soviet Union, however great the USSR's internal turmoil. In view of the split in Arab ranks resulting from the Iraq conflict, Syria may now be able to move ahead of the PLO, accept peace negotiations, and ignore the PLO's veto.

Helena Cobban is an experienced observer of the pertinent actors, including the Israelis, the Syrians, and the Palestinians. In this well-written and solidly researched paper, she describes and analyzes the interaction of these players within the context of their relations with both the United States and the Soviet Union.

To examine these relations anew has now become exceptionally important, for at least three reasons:

1. President Hafiz al-Asad of Syria, well known for his constant and skillful tactical maneuvers, has recently begun to make his peace with Egypt and has signaled that he may not want to become isolated, especially if the peace process were to show signs of life. Whether this is serious or yet another Syrian tactical move is difficult to say. Still, one cannot ignore the fact that the Syrian-Israeli frontier is the quietest of all and that Asad keeps his bargains once he has made them. Nor could one overlook the fact that Syria has something to gain from a successful peace process if it involved some solution for the disposition of the

Golan Heights. And Syria's participation in the anti-Saddam coalition has dealt Hafiz al-Asad powerful cards.

2. Israel's Prime Minister Yitzhak Shamir has made an important point in signaling a desire for direct negotiations with Syria. Whether he is only maneuvering to avoid direct Israeli-Palestinian talks, whether he merely wants to use the well-known hostility between Hafiz al-Asad and Yasir Arafat, or whether he just wants to highlight his argument that negotiations with Arab states have to come first (a highly impractical suggestion) should be left to the reader's analytical abilities.

3. The deep and notorious hostility between Hafiz al-Asad and Saddam Hussein is an important factor in view of Saddam's renewed attempts to assert Iraqi leadership in the Middle East, which led to the war of the anti-Saddam coalition against him. Conceivably it could make Asad more interested in the peace process, at least for the time being.

For all these reasons, Helena Cobban's insightful work is now especially timely and makes an indispensable contribution to those who seek greater understanding of the dangers and opportunities in the ever-explosive Middle East.

Robert G. Neumann
Senior Adviser
Director, Middle East Studies
The Center for Strategic and International Studies

About the Author

Helena Cobban, an analyst of Middle Eastern affairs, is scholar in residence at the Foundation for Middle East Peace. She has been a Social Science Research Council–MacArthur senior fellow in international peace and security studies at the University of Maryland's Center for International Security Studies as well as a guest scholar at the Brookings Institution. Editor of and contributor to *The Military Dimensions of Soviet Middle East Policy* (1988), she has published articles on the U.S.-Israeli strategic relationship and the implications of Israel's nuclear policy for the United States. Helena Cobban was coauthor, with Gerard C. Smith, of a 1989 article in *Foreign Affairs* on U.S. policy on nuclear nonproliferation. She is the author of *The Palestinian Liberation Organization: People, Power and Politics* (1984) and *The Making of Modern Lebanon* (1985).

Acknowledgments

This study would never have been possible without the generous support of the John D. and Catherine T. MacArthur Foundation, which funded three years of my work on it through the innovative Program in International Peace and Security Studies administered by the Social Studies Research Council in New York. I thank the MacArthur Foundation's Ruth Adams and the SSRC's Richard Rockwell for their particular encouragement for my work.

Coming from a Middle Eastern affairs background, I was lucky to be able to learn some of the principles of strategic analysis from gifted teachers at the University of Maryland's Center for International Security Studies at Maryland. These included Michael Nacht and Center director Catherine Kelleher, who gave me a welcoming home (and much-appreciated help from a research assistant) at Maryland for two years. Karen Dawisha, also of the University of Maryland, and Robert O. Freedman of Baltimore Hebrew University proved generous teachers and interpreters of Soviet affairs. The president of the Brookings Institution, Bruce MacLaury, and Foreign Policy Program Director John Steinbruner then gave me a Guest Scholar's position for a year and a half at Brookings, where William

Quandt, Michael MccGwire, and others contributed much from their various areas of expertise to the project. Ze'ev Schiff of *Ha'aretz*, Vitaliy Naumkin of the Soviet Institute of Oriental Studies, and Alexander George of Stanford University all made helpful contributions to strengthening the manuscript and to encouraging the author. Ann Hehr, Kathy Goldberg, and Roger Cressey gave valuable help at different stages of the research process, and all the librarians I encountered at the University of Maryland Graduate Library at College Park and at Brookings went out of their way to help me assemble the materials I needed. None of the above, however, bears any responsibility for inaccuracies or misjudgments in the work, for which I alone am accountable.

For all its shortcomings, I dedicate this study to my daughter, Lorna Quandt. I have been working on it for most of her young life, and she proved to be a great travel companion during research trips to Israel and Syria.

Perhaps one day she will pick this up and read it. I hope her world will be such that she asks in wonderment not only "What was the Cold War?" but also "What was the Syrian-Israeli conflict?"

Preface

The text of this volume was largely completed before Iraq's August 1990 invasion of Kuwait. That development and its early consequences changed the strategic architecture of much of the Middle East. Syria's incorporation into the U.S.-led alliance against Iraq and the collapse of the last vestiges of Soviet imperial reach meant that after August 1990 the Syrian-Israeli region was no longer buffeted by the bipolar superpower rivalry that dominated most of the preceding decade.

Even before August 1990, however, this work was designed as a historical case study of how things were in the Israel-Syria theater during the years 1978–1989, in an attempt to draw out lessons of value for the 1990s. It is with some relief that I note that all the analysis and nearly all the lessons identified in the text have retained their validity even after the sea change of August 1990! Indeed, many of the lessons identified herein—particularly those concerned with the urgency of reopening diplomatic efforts between Israel and Syria and the emerging opportunities toward this end—have been reinforced in their validity by the developments since August 1990.

Given the clarity of hindsight, much of how things were on the regional level from 1978 to 1989 already appeared at the time the text was completed to be an exercise in wasteful and destructive folly. This volume charts in some detail how, in the years following 1978, Israel maintained an excessively large military establishment that allowed General Ariel Sharon to try, in 1982, to pursue his dream of challenging Syria's position in the neighboring subtheater of Lebanon. The study shows how Sharon's adventure led to high human and economic losses and humiliation for Israel as well as Lebanon, while it spurred Syria into a large-scale arms buildup that gave Syria a rough reciprocity to the strategic deterrence that Israel had for years been able to project against Damascus.

On the international level, meanwhile, this study proposes the notion, which seemed bold when it was penned, that in the 1990s the Soviets might come to reverse their opposition, maintained since 1970, to any unilateral U.S. sponsorship of peace efforts in the Middle East and perhaps even come to view such an effort as the best chance for stabilizing a volatile region close to the Soviet Union's own southern borders. In December 1990, that notion already seems to have been overtaken by events: with massive unrest threatening their own heartland, today's Soviet rulers probably do not care much about anything in the Middle East at all, except insofar as it promises to affect their chances of putting bread on the tables of their people.

The events since August 1990 have changed a number of aspects of a Middle East that was already, as this volume shows, just starting to absorb the implications of the end of the global Cold War. As of the present writing, the Middle East seems somewhat closer to having the long-unfinished diplomatic business of Arab-Israeli peacemaking brought to an international conference than it was six months ago. At such a conference, or in any other forum where the parties try in good faith to resolve their differences, the question of bringing their overfull arsenals under some form of international control, and then reducing them, will occupy a central place. In pursuing this effort, negotiators must understand what lay behind the assembling of those arsenals in the first place. In the two important cases of Israel and Syria, it is hoped that this study contributes to such understanding.

Washington, D.C.
December 1990

Summary

This study analyzes strategic developments in the Israeli-Syrian region of the Middle East during the years 1978–1989 and the involvement of the United States and the Soviet Union in those developments. The peace treaty signed in 1979 between Israel and Egypt did not, as had been hoped, resolve Israel's conflicts with other major Arab states. Throughout the 1980s, both Israel and Syria devoted a high proportion of their national resources to preparing for a war against each other, while there was no sustained attempt to bring the conflict between them to the negotiating table.

During the decade that followed Camp David, Israel and Syria both significantly upgraded their strategic links with their respective superpower partners, which gave them access to more and better weapons than any the region had previously seen. During the early 1980s relations between Washington and Moscow became extremely tense, so the close strategic ties between the two Middle Eastern states and their respective superpower backers increased the probability that a major war between Israel and Syria would intentionally or unintentionally draw the superpowers into war.

The 1982 fighting between Israel and Syria in Lebanon revealed that a degree of mutual deterrence operated between them at that time, although the Israeli decision not to escalate in eastern Lebanon was apparently taken more in response to U.S. signals and Israeli domestic political factors than out of fear of Syrian reprisals. Then, after the 1982 fighting, Syria engaged in a military buildup that heightened the degree of deterrence it was able to project against Israel. For its part, Israel was easily able, throughout the period under study, to deter any offensive from Syria.

By the end of the 1980s, some Israeli decision makers, including Defense Minister Yitzhak Rabin, had shifted their rhetoric toward classic deterrence. Deterrence had still not been irreversibly adopted as Israel's national security doctrine, however. Meanwhile, the Syrians maintained the incentive to fight a war in the absence of any meaningful negotiations over the Golan. But Soviet restraint in arms transfers and in voicing commitments to Syria continued, along with Israel's effective projection of credible deterrent threats, to constrain the Syrian leadership from deciding to go to war. Thus, during the 1980s, local and international factors successfully combined to deter both sides from engaging in all-out warfare.

In its attempt to draw lessons about future prospects for stability in the Middle East, this study examines how tightened strategic links with local partners affected the decision making of the two superpowers. In the case of Washington's handling of its relationship with Israel, the emphasis shifted under President Reagan from a long-standing stress on "shared democratic values" to the strategic benefits the relationship could provide to the United States. This shift allowed Israel to argue throughout the 1980s that enhanced strategic links could be pursued regardless of disagreements in other spheres, including the Arab-Israeli peace process.

As tension between the superpowers relaxed toward the end of the decade, much of the U.S. rationale for enhancing strategic ties with Israel disappeared. Under President Bush, there were some preliminary indications that the relationship might be shifting back toward its former "moral" dimensions. This development could portend a closer link between the strategic and political strands of the relationship in the future.

On the Soviet side, the interests that the Soviets were pursuing through their relation with Syria stemmed from a mix of military and political motivations. The Soviets' stress on the relationship intensified in late 1982, after the United States had deployed an all-NATO force near Syrian positions in Lebanon.

After Mikhail Gorbachev came to power in 1985, he almost immediately started reining in Syria's military buildup. In April 1987, he delivered a clear message that his government would not support any Syrian attempt to initiate a war against Israel. Then, after the Soviet withdrawal from Afghanistan and the collapse of the Soviet empire in central Europe, it became impossible to consider that "maintaining the credibility of Soviet commitments" could still provide any rationale for Soviet support for Syria. Rather, the strategic concerns that the Gorbachev leadership continued to articulate concerning the Middle East began increasingly to center on the proliferation there of weapons of mass destruction and of missiles capable of reaching into Soviet territory. If these developments continue to be considered threatening in Moscow, there is a possibility that the Soviets might consider that the very Arab-Israeli *pax Americana* against which they fought for so long might provide one of the best means of enhancing their own national security.

The dyadic confrontation between Israel and Syria that marked the 1980s resulted primarily because Egypt had removed itself from the state of war with Israel, while Iraq's military attentions were focused eastward on the war against Iran. In 1988 the Iranians agreed to a cease-fire, and by early 1990 there was evidence that Iraq was seeking to return its attentions to the continuing conflict with Israel. It did this in competition with Syria, rather than in coalition with Syria. Yet the possibility that a regime change in either capital might lead to the establishment of a joint Iraqi-Syrian "Eastern front" could not be ruled out.

Policymakers approaching the challenge of Arab-Israeli peacemaking in the 1990s can learn useful lessons from the Israeli-Syrian confrontation of the 1980s. The most important of these concerns the urgency of moving the festering conflict between Israel and its neighbors into real negotiations that address the concerns of all the states and peoples involved. Deterrence cannot be stable over the long run in an environment in which major political differences remain unresolved. Meanwhile, the deadliness of the weapons systems acquired in the 1980s should have given all the parties increased motivation to find a way to resolve their differences without resorting to military confrontation.

Another major lesson concerns the increased possibility of finding technical solutions to previously intractable security problems. Israel's demonstration of a satellite-launch capability has opened up the new prospect that retaining occupied territories need no longer be considered essential to safeguard national security.

The Superpowers
and the
Syrian-Israeli
Conflict

1

The Context of the Syrian-Israeli Conflict, 1978–1989

Since the mid-1950s, the Arab-Israeli military conflict has had a strong capacity to affect the global balance of power. Until the mid-1970s, the major actor on the Arab side of this conflict was indisputably Egypt. But two disengagement agreements between Egypt and Israel, in 1973 and 1975, started to defuse the Egyptian-Israeli dimension of the conflict, and, through the Camp David accords of 1978, Egypt and Israel moved into a conflict resolution process that resulted in the signing of a formal peace treaty the following year. After Egypt left the confrontation, the major military dimension of the Arab-Israeli conflict became the conflict between Israel and Syria, a state of affairs that continued until the end of the 1980s.

The confrontation between Israel and Syria that dominated the Arab-Israeli region from 1978 through 1989 was characterized by numerous significant features. It was a confrontation in which the two superpowers maintained a high degree of involvement that each intensified and significantly formalized during the first half of the period under study. Thus, this confrontation risked drawing the superpowers directly into any shooting war that might break out between the local powers. It was also a confrontation, however, in which the local parties retained a considerable capacity to exert their own leverage over their superpower partners. In that regard, it differed from other regional conflicts, such as those in Afghanistan, Central America, southern Africa, or elsewhere, in which the engaged diplomacy of the superpowers was able, in the latter part of the 1980s, to register significant progress toward conflict resolution.[1]

Despite the absence, between 1978 and 1989, of any sustained diplomatic efforts aimed at resolving the long-standing conflict between Israel and Syria, this conflict nevertheless remained relatively stable throughout both the earliest part of that period (1978 through 1981), and then again throughout the latter years of the 1980s.[2] It was marked by a significant degree of instability only for the relatively brief period of 1981 through 1985.

What can account for these two phenomena—that is, the area's relative immunity to the diplomatic progress that marked other Third World conflicts in the late 1980s and the apparent stabilization of the situation even in the absence of such progress?

This study explores these questions initially through an examination of developments in this arena during the period from 1978 through 1989, and, subsequently, of the dynamics of the relationship each of the two superpowers maintained with its primary partner in the region. The study will explore the interactions within this quadrilateral of relationships, including the question of the relationship between the global political environment and the freedom of action of the local parties.

By early 1990, there were increasing signs that Syria's 12-year-old position as the major Arab state confronting Israel's military power was being challenged by Syria's neighbor to the east—Iraq. In a declaration on April 1, 1990, Iraq's President Saddam Hussein issued a pathbreaking deterrent threat against Israel, stating that if Israel should attempt to repeat its 1981 raid against the Iraqi nuclear reactor, then "by God, we will make fire eat up half of Israel."[3]

Significantly, in turning his belligerent attention back to Israel and away from the conflict with Iran to the east that had occupied him throughout the 1980s, Hussein made little attempt to join forces with a Syrian regime that still remained in a state of confrontation with Israel. Rather, at the political level, in early 1990 Hussein still challenged his longtime rivals in power in Syria. Thus, although the effects of Iraq's new anti-Israel stance caused new concern for Israeli planners, they seemed not to portend the imminent forging of an effective Syrian-Iraqi coalition, unless there should be major political changes in one of those two Arab capitals. Syria later joined the anti-Iraq coalition formed in response to Iraq's August 1990 invasion of Kuwait.

If Israel's military concerns should be spread, in the 1990s, from a situation in which the Syrian front was predominant to one in which the disparate military capabilities of both Syria and Iraq needed to be considered, a study of the experience of the essentially bipolar period of the 1980s might still provide valuable lessons. These lessons might be of interest to those concerned with regional stability as well as with the potential impact of instability in this region on global security in the more complex strategic world of the 1990s.

In many parts of the world, the early and mid-1980s were marked by an intensification of "regional" (that is, nonglobal) conflicts using relatively modern and deadly military technology. By the end of the decade, almost all of these conflicts were in the process of being resolved through political and diplomatic means. The exceptions were potentially the deadliest of them all—the conflicts between Israel and the Arab states and between India and Pakistan.

Few analysts, seeing the veritable waterfall of positive diplomatic developments in the Third World in the years between 1987 and 1989, failed to remark that they seemed to be connected with the concurrent relaxation of tensions between the United States and the Soviet Union. But how can we account for this apparent "trickle-down" effect? A possible explanation is the one favored by proponents of traditional cold war doctrines—namely, that the regional conflicts had all along been a function of global superpower rivalry and that, when this latter moved into a less confrontational mode, the superpowers decided to "turn off" the regional conflicts. An alternative explanation would stress the local factors and passions involved in the conflicts concerned. It would posit that those regional-level actors whose conflicts started moving toward resolution in the late 1980s would by then have reached the conclusion that their chances of continuing to draw their respective superpower patrons into their conflicts had diminished because of the new thaw in global politics. These actors would thus have decided to emphasize seeking local-level political means of resolving their conflicts and diminish their reliance on future battlefield victories. According to this explanation, the contribution of global powers to regional dynamics would not be so much in directly instigating, driving, or "turning off" regional conflicts, as in (less directly) fashioning the global political environment within which local actors made their own decisions on regional affairs.

The second explanation of "trickle down" from the global to the regional level seems more convincing than the first for three major reasons. First, despite the superpowers' powerful influence, fundamental decision-making power on issues of war and peace remained, for Third World conflicts, in the hands of the Third World states concerned. (This state of affairs is particularly a function of the postcolonial age, in which global powers are generally unable—in situations short of global war—to coerce local partners into peace or war.) In addition, the political antennae of most local actors as they consider the implications of global political factors for their own situations are very highly tuned—often much more acute, indeed, than the sensitivity of superpowers to regional-level dynamics. Finally, it is only this alternative explanation of "trickle down" that can, by ascribing due importance to local factors, adequately explain the failure or postponement of the move toward peaceful conflict resolution in the Syrian-Israeli situation.

As the experience of the first round of détente in the early 1970s amply demonstrated, the relationship between the state of superpower relations and regional conflict in the Third World is not a one-way street. Superpower relations – or, more precisely, expectations concerning trends in the same – affect the course of Third World conflicts; but the Third World conflicts themselves also greatly affect the state of superpower relations. Numerous Western analysts have charted the degree to which developments in the Middle East, southern Africa, and finally Afghanistan – and, more important, the Soviets' intervention in these areas – affected Western attitudes toward that round of détente. The Soviets have maintained that U.S. actions in the mid-1970s toward such Third World "hotbeds of tension" as Chile, the Horn of Africa, and the Middle East, have contributed to their own disillusionment with that détente.

If nearly all regional conflicts, however remote, potentially affect the state of superpower relations, then in no Third World region is this more apparent than in any portion of the Arab-Israeli arena. This truth is clearly indicated by the particular acuity of the global crises sparked by Arab-Israeli developments – an acuity that has been matched in the postwar history of the Third World only by the Cuban missile crisis of 1962, with its enormous risk of superpower confrontation.[4]

The susceptibility of the world political system to developments in the Arab-Israeli region has derived from a number of sources. Easiest to identify is the level of armament in this area, which rose rapidly from the late 1960s in both quantitative and qualitative terms, with periodic wars and near-wars propelling the arms-acquisition spiral as each side struggled to neutralize technical innovations revealed by its opponent in the previous round. By the mid-1980s, the extremely high technological level of the weapon systems available to both sides brought the military balance between them close to resembling, in some respects, that along the NATO–Warsaw Pact central front in Europe. It also – a crucial point in the present context – dramatically reduced the reaction time available to outside actors under most possible scenarios of a future full-scale engagement. Within this context of the continuing regional arms race, moreover, Israel's attainment in the late 1960s of a ready-to-use or quick-assembly nuclear capability gave it the capacity to exert extremely strong political leverage over both superpowers by being able to threaten the escalation of the conflict toward the nuclear threshold. (That such leverage may have been exerted over the United States during the 1973 Middle East war is indicated by some accounts of the period.)[5]

A second reason for the sensitivity of the global political system to developments in the Arab-Israeli conflict derives from the existence within the U.S. body politic of a well-organized constituency committed to its vision of Israel's welfare. The efficacy and awesome reputation of the pro-Israel "lobby" (in reality, a constellation of overlapping national and local organizations) made it impossible, in terms of U.S. decision making, to compare U.S.-Israeli relations and U.S. relations with any other country in the Third World, or perhaps with any other country anywhere. Throughout most of the 1980s, the pro-Israel lobby retained the influence in Washington that its organizers had been building continuously since the late 1950s. It was only at the end of the 1980s that, faced with the dilemmas posed by the uprising of Palestinians in the occupied territories, many of Israel's traditional friends in the United States began openly questioning the policies of the Israeli government. But by 1990, this *glasnost* in parts of the pro-Israel constituency was being expressed only with respect to Israel's policies toward the Palestinians; few perceptible questions were raised about Israel's policy toward Syria.

A third reason for the susceptibility of the world system to Arab-Israeli instabilities is that this region was generally, in the decades following the collapse of British imperial power in the Middle East, considered one in which the

two global superpowers each had strong strategic interests. The balance between these two competing assertions
of interest remained disputed, however. For the Soviets,
these interests derived primarily from the region's physical
proximity to their own southern borders. For the United
States, the Arab-Israeli region's close geographical and political relationship with the part of the world containing a
large proportion of the free world's proven oil reserves gave
it great strategic significance, as did both its proximity to
NATO's southern flank and the location within it of the
state of Israel.[6]

In a 1983 study, Alexander George described the dispute between the superpowers over the balance between
these interests in the following terms: "The Soviet Union,
implementing its claim to equality with the United States,
has tried unsuccessfully to get Washington to regard the
area as one of high-interest symmetry that requires a joint
U.S.-Soviet approach to peacemaking."[7] George, therefore,
characterized the relationship between the two superpowers in this area as "disputed interest symmetry."

The situation of "disputed interest symmetry" between
the superpowers made the Arab-Israeli arena one in which
the superpowers were more susceptible to being drawn into
crises originating at the local level than would, for example,
the situation George characterizes as marked by "high-
interest symmetry."[8] In 1967, 1970, 1973, and 1982–1983,
the eruption or escalation of fighting in the Arab-Israeli
theater confronted the superpowers with actual or potential global-level crises. In these crises, both Soviets and
Americans were guided by what George later called "the
basic rule of prudence in U.S.-Soviet relations . . . namely
that neither superpower shall initiate military action
against the forces of the other superpower." In spell-
ing out this rule, and some corollaries to it, George
stressed that they should be understood as "at most tacit
understandings and shared expectations that can be in-
ferred from patterns of behavior exhibited by Moscow and
Washington."[9]

Two corollaries that George introduced to his basic

rule of prudence (which were particularly relevant to the Arab-Israeli situation) were that "neither superpower shall permit a regional ally to drag it into a confrontation or shooting war with the other superpower" and that

> each superpower shall accept military intervention by the other superpower in a regional conflict if such inter-vention becomes necessary to prevent the overwhelm-ing defeat of a regional ally; moreover, in order to re-move the other superpower's incentive to intervene in such [a] situation each superpower shall accept respon-sibility for pressuring its regional ally to stop short of inflicting such a defeat on its local opponent.[10]

For his part, in an interview conducted in July 1988, the director of the USSR Ministry of Defense's official Military-History Institute, Colonel-General Dmitri Volko-gonov, displayed a roughly similar understanding of the informal "rules of prudence" governing superpower behav-ior in the Arab-Israeli theater. In the case of the Arab-Israeli war of 1973, Volkogonov noted that it had

> put both great powers in a difficult position. We had a moment when both the United States and the Soviet Union lost control of the situation, which was in the interests of neither. The United States and the Soviet Union both had an interest in stopping the conflict. . . . The factor of great power interests proved stronger than that of local powers.[11]

In the case of the June 1982 battles between the Syrian and Israeli forces in Lebanon, Volkogonov judged that, al-though relations between Moscow and Washington were tense at the time, "there was a political mechanism that prevented direct great power conflict." He stressed that he thought that the superpowers shared an interest in not seeing a total victory for either Israel or Syria in that conflict.[12]

Alexander George, in his analysis, expressed his recog-nition of "the superpowers' lack of perfect control over their regional allies . . . ."[13] In the case of the Arab-Israeli conflict, this lack of U.S. control over Israel in times of crisis was compounded by two of the factors mentioned above — namely, Israel's ability to exert a degree of nuclear-derived leverage over the United States and its influence within the U.S. political system, as well as by its ability to build up its own stockpiles of the weapons whose resupply would otherwise be a major means through which U.S. leverage could be exercised.

Would this conflict continue, in the 1990s, to be marked by a deep-seated dispute over the balance between the interests of the superpowers? In the latter years of the 1980s, there was some evidence that the Soviets might be rethinking the nature of their interests in the Middle East. The effects that such a Soviet reappraisal, as well as possible changes within the U.S.-Israeli relationship, might have on the prospects for war or peace in the Israel-Syria theater in the 1990s form part of the subject of the present inquiry.

This study explores the dynamics of the interaction between the local and global levels of the Syrian-Israeli military conflict in the years from 1978 through 1989. In keeping with the assessment that this conflict is driven primarily by local disagreements and only secondarily by the global relationship between the superpowers, the analysis will begin at the local level, building from that point to an analysis of the relationship between each of the two main actors and its superpower backer.

The study's geographic focus encompasses, whenever necessary, Israeli-Syrian confrontations in third areas such as Lebanon. It does not include the military balance between Israel and other potentially important Arab confrontation states such as Iraq. The tightness of this focus derives from two facts. First, throughout the period under study Syrian military power was the major threat to Israel's national security that was identified and anticipated by Israel's military tacticians; Iraq was occupied, meanwhile, by the punishing war against Iran; and other Arab armies were either too weak or too distant to deflect much Israeli attention from Syria. A second reason for the study's focus on the Israeli-Syrian component of the broader confrontation is that, throughout the 1980s, the effects on global politics of any major military confrontation between the two would have been particularly immediate and far-reaching.

The study's limited historical purview derives from the fact that in 1978 Egypt was effectively removed from the military balance in the Arab-Israeli conflict. This is not to deny the contribution that Egypt continued to make to Arab-Israeli regional dynamics after 1978, particularly in questions concerning the essentially political (rather than military) contest between Israelis and Palestinians. Nor is it to deny the possibility that Egypt may one day return its relatively vast bulk to the Arab side of a military confrontation with Israel. At the end of the 1980s, however, that day still seemed far off. Indeed, such a contingency would spark a large-scale crisis for U.S. policy-making in the area long before any effective Egyptian troops could reach the international border with Israel. The "Egypt factor" is, at best, only obliquely relevant to the purview of this study. Egypt-related considerations are introduced as necessary, however, in examining the lessons of past Arab-Israeli crises, in examining past Soviet behavior in the region, and in assessing the future prospects for moving the Israeli-Syrian conflict or other portions of the Arab-Israeli conflict into a meaningful negotiation.

The probability of a war between Syria and Israel had not been constant throughout the years under study. Chapter 2 charts the shifts in the probability of full-scale Israeli-Syrian war over this period—a probability that initially reached a relatively high plateau lasting from about 1981 through 1985 and then decreased beginning in 1986. (As noted previously, one aim of the present inquiry is to explain the latter phenomenon.)

The strategic linkages between each of these two governments and its superpower partner are the subjects of chapters 3 and 4. In the years following 1978, these linkages both became much tighter than formerly. In October 1980 Syria concluded its first formal Treaty of Friendship and Cooperation with the Soviet Union. The increase in the level of operational cooperation between the two parties then sharply accelerated in the 1982–1983 period when an estimated 6,000 Soviet military personnel were deployed to Syria. (That number later diminished. In mid-1989, it was estimated at 3,000.)[14]

In the case of Israel, in 1981 its government concluded a Memorandum of Understanding (MOU) on strategic collaboration with the United States. That first MOU was suspended by the United States before the end of 1981, but in November 1983 the U.S. administration reinstated the formal strategic cooperation between the two sides at a new, higher level. In the following years, strategic collaboration between these two parties encompassed an ever-increasing number of fields of strategic activity, which included, at the more exotic end of the spectrum, joint work on the Strategic Defense Initiative (SDI). At the more mundane end, the United States started building stockpiles of prepositioned combat matériel in Israeli territory, the U.S. and Israeli navies conducted a number of joint exercises in the eastern Mediterranean in the years following 1983, and U.S. Navy pilots started conducting regular bombing practice at test sites inside Israel. The chances of local parties dragging the superpowers into their confrontation only seemed to be increased by these developments.

Chapter 5 then draws conclusions about the nature of the interaction between the global and local powers in the Syria-Israel theater between 1978 and 1989, about which factors best explain both the immunity of this area to the global trend toward peaceful resolution of regional conflicts in the later years of the 1980s, and about the stabilization that occurred even in the absence of active peace-making.

THE PERIOD BEING STUDIED was one in which the relationship between the two superpowers evidenced great dynamism. The year 1978 has been aptly characterized by Raymond Garthoff as marking "a turn toward confrontation."[15] The potential for confrontation between the two superpowers further deepened after the Soviets' December 1979 invasion of Afghanistan and the Americans' election of Ronald Reagan as president the following year. In 1983 Reagan announced his Strategic Defense Initiative and articulated the so-called Reagan doctrine of attempting to roll back Soviet gains in the Third World. In September 1983 the Soviets shot down a civilian Korean airliner, which apparently confronted policymakers in both superpower capitals with the potential danger of a war's starting by accident or miscalculation. Beginning in the spring of 1984, both superpowers seemed to be searching for a way to lessen the intense confrontation that characterized their relationship. The relaxation in U.S.-Soviet tensions continued through six summit-level meetings between November 1985 and December 1989, the signing of the INF treaty in December 1987, and considerable progress toward resolving a host of other problems that had previously plagued the relationship.[16]

The activism in foreign affairs of General-Secretary (later President) Mikhail Gorbachev was by no means limited to U.S.-Soviet issues; it also resulted in a dramatic rethinking of Soviet policies toward a number of Third World issues. The most clearcut instance of this occurred in Afghanistan, where Gorbachev initiated a total withdrawal of combat troops that was completed according to schedule in February 1989. Elsewhere in the Third World, Soviet pressure on local allies was also a significant factor in moving the long-standing conflicts in southern Africa and Cambodia toward negotiated resolutions. Would an analogous rethinking of Soviet commitments also occur concerning Soviet-Syrian relations? There were, as will be noted, some indications that this question was starting to be addressed, however obliquely, in the Kremlin beginning in 1987; the signals of caution from that quarter were among the causes of the relative stability that the Syria-Israel theater evinced in those years.[17]

It should also be noted that the relationships that the two superpowers maintained with their principal allies in the Israel-Syria theater were not completely exclusive.

Throughout most of the post–Camp David period, the United States maintained active diplomatic contacts with Damascus, which exhibited their own dynamic of ebb and flow. (Indeed, U.S. communications with Damascus played an important role in limiting the summer 1982 crisis.) And in Gorbachev's Moscow, one part of the "new thinking" on the Middle East was translated into a cautious diplomatic opening to Israel beginning in 1987.

To assess the prospects for the coming decade, Chapter 5 therefore also draws together the lessons from all these changes in the Israeli-Syrian-U.S.-Soviet quadrilateral during the 1980s. How might the trends in the relationship between the global and local levels of the conflict affect the ability of outside powers to respond effectively to the military crisis that still, at the start of the decade, remained a possibility? Or, how might they affect the possibility that, in the years ahead, the Syrian-Israeli conflict and all other remaining parts of the Arab-Israeli conflict might be led away from military preparations and into a meaningful negotiation?

2

Developments in the Conflict

The Syrian-Israeli Conflict in
the Post–Camp David Period

From 1978 through 1989, Syria and Israel were locked into a complex confrontational relationship in which each described the other as the major military threat to its own security or even to its national existence.[1] The Syrians' complaints against Israel centered on the Israeli occupation since 1967 of a strip of Syrian national territory atop the Golan Heights and on the fear that a militarily superior Israel might launch a repeat of its stunning 1967 destruction of the Syrian armed forces. Israel's complaint against Syria centered on the fear that, not content with regaining Golan, the Syrians still sought the destruction of the Jewish state.

To support these alarming claims, each side was able to indicate a broad array of actions undertaken by the other government as well as bellicose statements emanating from its capital. Other presumably more authoritative statements from both sides, such as the commitment they both professed to United Nations (UN) Security Council

Resolution 242 mandating a return of territories occupied in 1967 in exchange for ending the state of war, might have indicated that cautious diplomacy could reduce the mistrust between them.

Concerning Israel's intentions, successive Israeli governments have always spelled out their readiness to make peace with Syria—the major question has been on what terms they would do so, and in particular, whether they would be prepared to trade any significant amount of the occupied Golan Heights for a real peace agreement with Syria. The true intentions of Syria's ruler since 1970, President Hafiz al-Asad, are more difficult to gauge. The 1988 assessment of Patrick Seale, a veteran and generally sympathetic observer of Syrian affairs, was that the future vision of Asad's Syria was for "a balance of power between an Arab Levant centered on Damascus and an Israel within its 1948–1949 boundaries."[2] Although this vision may have seemed acceptable to few in Israel, it certainly implied a Syrian readiness to coexist with an Israel of continuing vitality.

Throughout the period under study, however, there were no serious efforts by either of the parties, or by their superpower friends, to probe the possibility of a diplomatic resolution of their conflict. Indeed, as far as the U.S. government position was concerned, it appeared to continue, throughout this period, to consider itself bound by an undertaking President Gerald Ford had spelled out to Israel's then-Premier Yitzhak Rabin in a conversation in September 1974 and reconfirmed in a written Memorandum of Agreement one year later. Ford had written that, although the United States had not yet developed a final position on the location of Israel's final border with Syria, "should it do so it will give great weight to Israel's position that any peace agreement with Syria must be predicated on Israel remaining on the Golan Heights." Ford also promised Rabin that "should the U.S. desire in the future to put forward proposals of its own, it will make every effort to coordinate with Israel its proposals with a view to refraining from putting forth proposals that Israel would consider unsatisfactory."[3]

Between 1978 and 1989, the contest between Israel and Syria was, therefore, played out through primarily military rather than diplomatic means—through opposing troop deployments on the Golan as well as in the two subsidiary arenas of Lebanon and the eastern Mediterranean. It was also pursued through both sides' continued acquisition of "strategic" deep-penetration capabilities that included bomber aircraft, surface-to-surface missiles, and the ability to arm them with chemical warheads (in the case of Syria), or (in the case of Israel) chemical or nuclear warheads.

By the end of the 1980s, some Israeli commentators were starting to shed the veils of opacity in which Israel's nuclear capabilities had previously been shrouded.[4] By then, too, Israeli defense officials and civilian commentators were starting to use the language of the superpowers' deterrence relationship to describe their own relationship with Syria (see the last section in this chapter). The nonconventional military capabilities that underpinned this Israeli-Syrian deterrence relationship had existed for some years prior to 1978. Until nearly the end of the period covered by the present study, each side kept its arsenal of nonconventional weapons under wraps that were sufficiently opaque to avoid action by the superpowers or other international actors to dismantle or control them. Nevertheless, the nonconventional capabilities of both sides were sufficiently visible to each other that they must be judged to have defined the broad strategic environment in which the two governments pursued their decision making in national security affairs.

During the period under study, the principal land front, on Golan, remained absolutely calm. The disengagement agreement that U.S. Secretary of State Henry Kissinger negotiated for Golan in 1974 remained stably in force thereafter, under the supervision of the United Nations Disengagement Observer Force (UNDOF), which maintained a thin buffer between the zones of Israeli and Syrian control on the Golan. From their front lines, the Israel Defense Forces (IDF) maintained positions 50 kilometers (30 miles) from downtown Damascus across a gently sloping plain. In the early years of UNDOF's existence, the Syrians exercised some political brinksmanship by seeking to reopen the negotiations on the long-term status of Golan whenever the question of renewing UNDOF's mandate arose. As the years passed, however, Asad abandoned even these halfhearted efforts. In December 1981, in a move that stopped just short of explicit annexation, the Israeli government unilaterally extended the jurisdiction of its laws to Golan. That action caused some temporary strain in Israel's relations with Washington (see chapter 3), but it failed to affect Syria's continued compliance with the UNDOF regime.

The naval dimension of the Syrian-Israeli contest assumed increasing importance during the decade under study. Both Israel and Syria were diverting an increased proportion of their defense expenditures into naval acquisitions, and it was in the realm of naval planning in the eastern Mediterranean that some of the closest interactions developed between these local parties and their respective superpower partners. During the decade following Camp David, the Israelis increased their missile-boat force and upgraded their shipborne missile systems. In 1988 they contracted with a West German shipyard to add three conventionally fueled submarines to double their submarine inventory. For their part, the Syrians greatly improved their coastal defenses in this period; they also acquired three R-class submarines and 12 antisubmarine warfare helicopters.[5] Arab press reports, meanwhile, occasionally referred to naval engagements near the Syrian coast that appeared to be connected to continuing Israeli attempts to probe Syria's coastal defenses.[6]

As of late 1989, the two sides' new naval assets had not been tested in any direct confrontation. Such naval activity as there had been through that point was limited

to Israel's naval and amphibious operations around the
coast of Lebanon, but these never provoked any resistance
from a Syria that seemed to countenance Israel's sea-based
operations in an area that extended to Lebanon's northern
border. Then, in the spring and summer of 1989, Syrian
boats moved near to the Lebanese shore in an area stretch-
ing northward from Beirut in a largely successful attempt
to impose a naval blockade on dissident Christian forces
there. On this occasion, Israel's navy made no attempt to
intervene; Israeli military sources signaled that they saw
no threat to Israel in this situation.[7] In any future all-out
clash between the two states, however, there would be a
great potential for naval engagements. These could, as happened during the 1973 war, take the war to Syria's coastal
cities. They could also, because of the two superpowers'
naval presence in the region and their increasingly close
operational links with the naval forces of their respective
local partners, rapidly draw the superpowers to the heart
of any confrontation between the Israeli and Syrian navies.

With the Golan front quiet, the naval "front" untested,
and no decision by either side to unveil or employ the strategic, heartland-busting capabilities at its disposal, the military contest between Israel and Syria during the post–
Camp David decade was played out almost entirely in Lebanon. Lebanon had been wracked by civil and international
strife since 1975, when the fragile regime that was regulating relations between its five major population groups
started to unravel. At the heart of the Lebanese conflict
was the failure of these groups to agree on how to coexist
within Lebanon's tight, mountain-dominated confines,
which invited the intervention of virtually any self-interest-
ed outsider who might care to establish an alliance with
some combination of Lebanese actors. As generations of
outsiders from Nebuchadnezzar onward had discovered,
such intervention involved its own costs and risks. Nevertheless, in the years following 1975, both Israel and Syria
were drawn ever further into what veteran Israeli military
writer Ze'ev Schiff has called "the Lebanese bear-hug."[8]

Both Israel and Syria had some genuine national security concerns stemming from the volatile situation in Lebanon. On both sides, however, official declaratory policy also helped to push these governments further into the Lebanese game. For the Syrian leaders, there were real national security goals to be met in eastern Lebanon, which forms a natural invasion route for forces seeking to attack Damascus from the south or west. They also felt, however, an occasional need to be seen to be confronting "the Zionist threat" somewhere on earth, although they never chose to do so on their own turf in the Golan. For the Israelis, meanwhile, there was concern for the vulnerability of communities in northern Israel to the guerrillas operating from south Lebanon. In addition, there was also a strong political push to take visible action against the worldwide "terrorist threat," even after a cease-fire concluded for south Lebanon in spring 1978 proved to be surprisingly durable. For both Israel and Syria, the most cost-free arena in which to pursue these multiple agendas was judged to be Lebanon.

With both of these outsiders barreling about in Lebanon in pursuit of these partly political, partly military aims, it was almost inevitable that they might occasionally barrel right into each other. It is important to note, however, that the aims of their interventions in Lebanon were often parallel, as in their shared opposition to the 1976 PLO-leftist coalition, rather than always contradictory. In most instances, the Israeli and Syrian agendas in Lebanon actually included an admixture of shared and mutually contradictory goals. Through the development of an implicit understanding between the two leaderships, one of the shared goals came to be that neither would allow developments in Lebanon to drag it against its volition into all-out war against the other. (The two parties thus to some degree replicated, in the subordinate Lebanese arena, tacit rules similar to those that the superpowers had evolved for the Third World, as noted in chapter 1.)

The applicability of this rule was not a foregone conclusion, and it was subject to particularly rigorous testing during the Israeli invasions of Lebanon of 1978 and 1982. In March 1978 the Israelis committed 25,000 troops to an invasion of south Lebanon called the "Litani Operation." But, as Israeli analyst Yair Evron has attested, during this operation, "Israel was careful to signal to Syria that the battle was not directed at it, that the objectives of the operation were limited, and that there was no need for it to intervene."[9] The Syrians' response was cautious: President Hafiz al-Asad opted to wait out the Israeli action and take whatever losses were involved in Lebanon. He decided neither to throw all Syria's strategic weight into that arena in response to the Israeli action, nor to open up any of the other fronts in his ongoing contest with Israel. In 1982, as will be evident later, his reaction was correspondingly cautious, although the level of confrontation was much higher. On both occasions, Asad's actions clearly signaled that he was not going to be provoked, by events in Lebanon, into a war decision that was not of his own choosing.

For their part, the Israelis generally responded to the threat posed by the Palestinian guerrilla organizations with massive punitive or preemptive raids against guerrilla concentrations and logistical facilities in Lebanon. These raids notably did not include retaliations against Syrian territory, even when there was evidence of Syrian complicity with the guerrillas.

The caveat noted above that neither party allowed itself to be dragged against its volition into all-out war against the other could make implementing the understanding between them difficult in practice, because the absence of any direct diplomatic contacts meant that one or the other of them might not know when the volition of the other might suddenly have changed. Clearly, something more than indirect signaling was required, particularly as the direct entanglement of both parties in Lebanon increased beginning in 1976. What emerged, with Syria's first large-scale deployment of troops to Lebanon in spring 1976, was a series of understandings between the two governments negotiated through the good offices of the U.S. government. (The fact of this sponsorship was reportedly one of the reasons for Soviet opposition between 1976 and 1982 to Syria's presence in Lebanon.)

These understandings, whose net effect was to allow but to regulate Syria's direct intervention in Lebanon, came to be known as the Red Lines agreements. According to Ze'ev Schiff, the Red Lines represented three features: Syria would not deploy ground-to-air missiles in Lebanon; the Syrian air force would not operate against Christian objectives in Lebanon; and the Syrian ground forces would not move south from Sidon to Mashghara (in eastern Lebanon).[10]

Throughout the year that followed the Syrian army's deployment into Lebanon in spring 1976, a series of further communications and actions was undertaken to fine-tune the application of the Red Lines understandings, and they thereafter proved extremely durable.[11] Their durability was particularly remarkable considering that the political nature of each side's involvement in Lebanon evolved over the years following 1976 to include (as previously noted) some elements of competition as well as some parallel interests. In addition, the Israelis used their overall strategic superiority in Lebanon (including their uncontested control of Lebanese airspace and coastal waters) to continue launching heavy raids against suspected PLO positions in areas of Lebanon still under Syrian control. Nevertheless, as we shall see, the Red Lines understandings remained in place through 1981 and were restored virtually intact in Lebanon from 1985 on.

Israel's Strategic Position from the Mid-1970s through 1981

In the Camp David accords of September 1978, Israel and Egypt agreed to conclude a peace treaty, which they did in March 1979. The treaty delineated a three-year timetable, under which successive phases of Israel's withdrawal from occupied Sinai would be matched with phases of Egypt's normalization of relations with Israel. Full withdrawal would be matched with full normalization in April 1982. Thereafter, Sinai would become substantially demilitarized, under the supervision of a U.S.-led grouping called the Multinational Force and Observers (MFO).

So long as this regime lasted, Israel would be guarded from surprise attack from Egypt by the following elements: the 180-kilometer (110-mile) buffer of the Sinai desert; the reporting of the MFO and continued U.S. aerial monitoring that would be reported to both sides; the Israeli and U.S. presence in Egypt that resulted from the treaty; and the constraints placed on Egypt's freedom of action by the arms-supply relationship with the United States that stemmed from Egypt's participation in the peace process.[12]

Implementation of the treaty went ahead according to schedule, removing from the Arab-Israeli military balance the weightiest of the Arab countries along Israel's borders. This development came, moreover, after the disengagement agreements of 1973 and 1975 had already substantially reduced the risk of a resumption of war between Egypt and Israel.[13]

The reduction of the threat from Egypt that resulted from Camp David was epoch-making for Israel. It did not, however, lead Israel's national-security decision makers to reduce their standing army from the high levels that had been maintained since the October 1973 war. Indeed, the size of the full-time and reserve components of the Israel Defense Force manpower both rose slightly between 1977 and 1981 (see table 1). Between 1978 and 1980, Israel's annual defense expenditures did shrink somewhat in absolute terms – a shrinkage that was more pronounced when expressed as a proportion of gross domestic product or GDP (see figures 1 and 2). But they still remained considerably higher than the levels that had prevailed before the 1973 war. And in 1981, defense expenditures rose sharply once again, exceeding 1978's total in both absolute and rela-

TABLE 1

Armed Forces of Israel and Syria as Proportion of the Population, 1977–1989 (in thousands)

	1977	1979	1981	1983	1985	1987	1989
Israel							
A. Total population	3,622.0	3,820.0	4,000.0	4,100.0	4,300.0	4,450.0	4,542.0
B. Numbers in regular armed forces	164.0	165.6	172.0	172.0	142.0	141.0	141.0
C. Numbers in reserves	460.0	460.0	504.0	326.0	370.0	504.0	504.0
D. Manpower burden of reserve (C/12)	38.3	38.3	42.0	27.2	30.8	42.0	42.0
E. Total defense manpower burden (B + D)	202.3	203.9	214.0	199.2	172.8	183.0	183.0
F. Defense manpower as proportion of population (E/A) (percent)	5.6	5.4	5.4	4.9	4.0	4.1	4.0
Syria							
A. Total population	7,750.0	8,370.0	9,150.0	9,200.0	11,000.0	11,250.0	11,724.0
B. Numbers in regular armed forces	227.5	227.5	222.5	222.5	402.5	407.5	404.0
C. Numbers in reserves	102.5	102.5	102.5	102.5	272.5	272.5	400.0
D. Manpower burden of reserve (C/12)	8.5	8.5	8.5	8.5	22.7	22.7	33.3
E. Total defense manpower burden (B + D)	236.0	236.0	231.0	231.0	425.2	430.2	437.3
F. Defense manpower as proportion of population (E/A) (percent)	3.0	2.8	2.5	2.5	3.9	3.8	3.7

Source: The Military Balance (London: International Institute for Strategic Studies), for various years.

23

MCKINSTRY LIBRARY
LINCOLN COLLEGE
LINCOLN, ILLINOIS

FIGURE 1
Annual Defense Expenditures of Israel and Syria, 1975–1988 (in constant 1980 dollars)

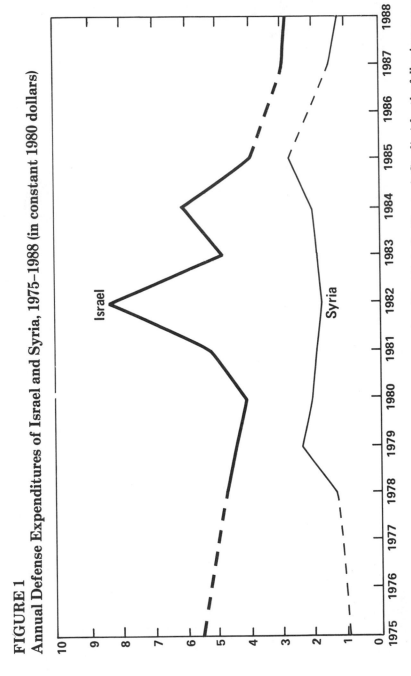

Source: Data from *The Military Balance* (London: International Institute for Strategic Studies) for the following years: *1987–1988,* pp. 217–218, and *1989–1990,* p. 209.

FIGURE 2

Defense Expenditures of Israel and Syria as a Percentage of Gross Domestic Product, 1975–1989

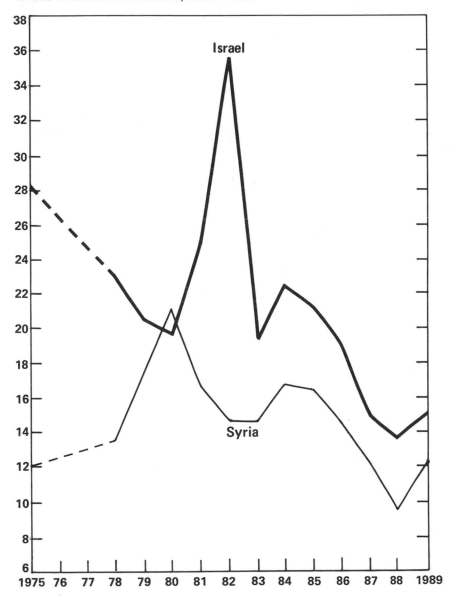

Source: See *The Military Balance* for the following years: *1987-1988*, pp. 217–218; *1988-1989*, p. 225; *1989-1990*, p. 102, 209; and *1990-1991*, p. 106, 118.

25

tive terms. Meanwhile, the manpower figures still indicated
that, between the conclusion of the Camp David accords
and the middle of 1982, the Israelis made no decision to
respond to the lessening of the threat from Egypt by standing down any proportion of the country's substantial order
of battle.

This nondecision by the Israelis contrasted strikingly
with the policy that Israel's founding father, Prime Minister David Ben-Gurion, had adopted in the early 1950s. In
that earlier era, Ben-Gurion decided that, because the 1949
Armistice Agreements between Israel and its Arab neighbors had already substantially stabilized Israel's strategic
situation, economic and social development were more important priorities for the infant Jewish state than defense
spending. He therefore decided to cut the defense budget
substantially, dismissing thousands of IDF regulars and
defense sector civilians.[14] Ben-Gurion made that decision
(which proved, in retrospect, to have been a wise one) at a
time when the state of war with Israel's Arab neighbors
still existed, although it was tempered by the Armistice
Agreements. Yet, his Israel had nothing like a formal peace
treaty with Egypt to rely on. In the aftermath of Camp
David, by contrast, few voices were heard in Israel arguing
that the country was now in a position to make an analogous strategic reapportionment of national resources. One
of those who did press this argument was the head of the
Foreign Ministry's intelligence department, Zvi Lanir, who
had a long history in Israel's intelligence community.[15] But
Ben-Gurion's successor in the political leadership decided
not to take this advice. Why?

Three factors probably contributed to this nondecision. The first was the fact that by the late 1970s, much of
the direct cost of the Israeli defense establishment was
being met not from Israel's own revenues but from U.S.
aid. The second was that political inertia, in the absence of
any such urgent social problems as those that plagued the
state in the early 1950s, allowed the defense establishment
to continue with "business as usual." And the third was

that, long after the guns of the 1973 Arab-Israeli war fell silent, the Israeli public continued to reel from the trauma caused by the ability the Arab states had shown to achieve virtually complete strategic surprise.

In the aftermath of the 1973 war, while an official Israeli commission was investigating the causes of the intelligence failure, IDF planners set about trying to ensure that never again would they be at a loss in dealing with a surprise Arab offensive. Over the five years that followed 1973, the standing forces were increased by about 50 percent over their prewar level, and the reserve force was more than doubled. The readiness and mobility of most parts of the IDF were increased, and ammunition stocks were multiplied. Technological improvements were introduced across a broad spectrum of the IDF's capabilities; interarm coordination and other aspects of command, control, communication, and intelligence (C^3I) were upgraded to state-of-the-art levels.[16] Needless to say, all of these steps had required a huge increase in defense spending—roughly double the level of the early 1970s.

The high defense expenditures of the mid- and late 1970s coincided with a period in which deep structural trends were advancing new political forces in Israel. In 1977 national elections brought to power the ultranationalist Likud bloc, which had spent the first 29 years of Israeli statehood in opposition to the Labor Party. From 1977 through the end of the 1980s, the Likud would remain a dominant force in the Israeli government, though the elections of 1985 and late 1988 both resulted in coalitions in which Likud was joined by Labor. The Likudniks and their predecessors in the Revisionist Zionist movement had always placed more emphasis than Labor on the role of force in implementing their objectives. The rise of Likud probably helped to ensure that little official consideration was given, in the aftermath of the Camp David accords, to the idea of standing down some of the country's armed forces.

After 1978 there remained in Israel a perception of a continued threat in which Syria now came to play the dominant role. The immediacy of this threat could have remained open to some question. After all, at the end of the 1973 war, the Israelis had nearly reached Damascus. Then, throughout the mid-1970s, the Syrians stuck rigidly to the terms of the 1974 disengagement agreement, and from 1976 on they showed a surprising readiness to coordinate their actions in Lebanon with Israel. Syria's defense spending meanwhile lagged considerably behind that of Israel.

Nevertheless, cultural and historical factors combined with the aforementioned political factors to pressure Israel's military planners to err on the side of excessive caution. For them, as for many Israelis, the struggle with Syria seemed to be not merely a border dispute but, rather, an existential battle for the survival of the Jewish people in its ancient homeland. Those in Israel who evinced serious concern about the threat from the northeast could, moreover, point to a number of alarming indicators of its magnitude: to Syria's 3 : 2 superiority in the numbers of its regular forces (see table 1); to any one of a series of belligerently anti-Israel speeches by Syrian leaders; or to the possibility of a combination of hostile Arab forces gathering along the Syrian border for another surprise attack.[17]

In their public rhetoric throughout the 1970s, Israeli leaders from both major parties also made frequent reference to the threat from terrorism. Although at this time terrorism never posed a major threat to Israeli national security, the high priority that Israeli declaratory policy accorded it, and the accompanying policy of massive retaliation against the sources from which it emanated, had a significant effect on military planning and operations with respect to Lebanon. Because Lebanon was one of the most important arenas in Israel's ongoing confrontation with Syria, as well as being a country with which the United States enjoyed strong traditional ties of friendship, Israel's retaliatory policy also affected its relations with both of those important parties.

Throughout the 1970s, the major targets of Israel's antiterrorist policy in Lebanon were the logistics bases of the various Palestinian guerrilla groups headquartered there. From Lebanon, the guerrillas launched sporadic, much-publicized forays into northern Israel. In May 1974, for example, three members of the Democratic Front for the Liberation of Palestine (DFLP) gained control of a school building in the northern town of Ma'alot, taking hostage a group of Israeli teenagers. When attempts were made to rescue the hostages, the guerrillas executed 21 of them before falling to the attackers' fire. In March 1978, 35 Israelis and 6 guerrillas from the Fateh organization were killed in a similar incident in Tel Aviv.

These and many other Palestinian guerrilla operations provoked a heavy Israeli response in the form of air raids or naval bombardments against suspected guerrilla positions in Lebanon, resulting in a ratio of casualties highly unfavorable to the Palestinians. After the March 1978 incident, the IDF committed approximately 25,000 troops to an invasion of south Lebanon that it dubbed the Litani Operation. This left the IDF in control of nearly the whole of south Lebanon up to the Litani River. (The Syrian army occupied positions close to the IDF's final front line, but on that occasion the Syrians chose not to fight.) Under pressure from the United States, the Israelis withdrew their forces from nearly all the occupied area between April and June 1978; they remained only in a 10-kilometer-wide security zone immediately north of the border, where they now consolidated under IDF command some ragtag local Christian militias.

The Litani Operation left two important legacies in Israeli planning. After it, Israel had a much greater and more direct role than ever before in the continuing imbroglio of Lebanese politics. Israel also established the possibility of conducting large-scale operations in Lebanon without unduly straining the relationship with the United States.[18]

The relationship with Washington had been a key component of Israeli strategic planning since the 1967 Arab-Israeli war, when the United States emerged as Israel's major source of both high-technology weapons and international political support. In the fighting of 1973, many Israelis had been unpleasantly surprised by the rapidity with which the IDF consumed its military supplies. One of the key decisions made after the war was, as noted above, to increase readiness by building up the size of the available stockpiles. The increased stockpiles would also, not coincidentally, give the Israelis more freedom of action from Washington in future military crises. Still, some Israeli strategic thinkers concluded from the experience of 1973 that in the era of high-technology warfare Israel's dependence on the goodwill of its outside supplier had been unavoidably increased.[19] So, too, in the international isolation Israel suffered in the years following 1973, had its dependence on U.S. political support.

Israel's international position improved somewhat after the conclusion of the Camp David accords, though its failure to follow through on the Palestinian part of the accords led to some later erosion in its international standing. Ronald Reagan's inauguration as U.S. president in January 1981, however, ushered in a new period of unprecedented official U.S. support for Israel (see chapter 3). Although this development was considered a great boon by most Israeli decision makers, it also enabled Israel to continue to avoid making tough national-strategic choices analogous to those that Ben-Gurion had made in the early 1950s.

In 1981, however, this negative effect of the advent of the new U.S. administration was still not foreseeable. In April 1981, Reagan's secretary of state, Alexander Haig, made a visit to Israel. By the time he left, according to Ze'ev Schiff and Ehud Ya'ari, "there was no doubt in many minds that with a man of Haig's bent running the State Department, Israel could definitely allow itself to adopt a militant posture vis-à-vis Damascus."[20]

Syria's Position after Camp David

If the conclusion of the Camp David accords afforded Israel an opportunity (whether exploited or not) to enjoy some strategic respite, for Syria it only raised the level of the perceived threat. Egypt was now effectively removed from the strategic equation with Israel; Jordan could be presumed to derive some protection from Israeli attack from its close relationship with the United States; and there was no continuing peace process under way that might lead to some hope of resolving the Israel-Syria issue. The Syrians thus expressed many fears that Israel's entire strategic weight might now be directed against their own positions in Syria or in Lebanon.

When Sadat had introduced his peace initiative with Israel in 1977, the first reaction of Syrian President Hafiz al-Asad had been to try to form a coalition of all those Arab governments that opposed it. At that stage, Asad was able to line up four partners in what became known as the Steadfastness Front (Jabhat al-Sumoud wat-Tasaddi) – Algeria, South Yemen, Libya, and the PLO. Of these partners, however, only the PLO fielded any forces along the front line with Israel, and they were of little help to the Syrians both because of their relatively small size and because of their entanglement in the often hostile Lebanese environment. Moreover, the PLO's objectives in Lebanon were frequently at odds with those of Syria, as was shown during numerous clashes between the two forces there beginning in 1976.

The major contribution that the 1977 Steadfastness Front made to bolstering Syrian security was the support that Algeria and Libya gave to the Syrian defense budget. After the Camp David accords were signed the following year, Syria's ability to put together a meaningful coalition of Arab states substantially increased, because a number of other Arab states now moved into the anti-Egypt coalition. The most strategically significant of these was Iraq, which had a serious military capability that might, after further joint planning, be brought into effective action along Syria's border with Israel.

The process of Iraqi-Syrian reconciliation never reached that point. The two countries were ruled by factions of the Arab Socialist Renaissance (Ba'th) Party that had been bitterly at odds since 1963. In the dictatorial system of single-party domination that was a hallmark of Ba'thist rule, the relations between the two states continued to be a function of relations between the two parties; at this level, the rivalry was too deep to be overcome. In July 1979 news emerged of an intraparty feud in the Iraqi capital, Baghdad. The country's longtime Ba'thist strongman, Saddam Hussein, elbowed his way into the presidency and launched a bloody purge against those of his colleagues suspected of being too keen on the reconciliation with Syria. Relations between the two states returned to their former hostile stance, which was only further exacerbated when Syria supported Iran in the Iran-Iraq War of 1980–1988.

One other legacy of 1978's broad anti-Sadat front provided a more durable contribution to Syria's defense effort. This was the increased Arab funding pledged to the "frontline" states by the Arab summit held in Baghdad in November 1978. Of the annual total pledged by the oil-exporting states, $1.8 billion was earmarked for Syria.[21] Although several of the Arab funders reneged on their pledges over the years that followed, the effect of Steadfastness Front and Baghdad summit contributions can be seen in the increase registered in Syrian defense spending from 1979 on (see figure 1). In the years before 1979, Syrian defense spending had remained more or less stable at a level of just over U.S. 1980 $1 billion—between one-fifth and one-quarter of the Israeli levels.[22] There was then a definite spike in 1979, after which the annual figure stabilized once again, this time at a level roughly double the pre-1979 level.

Despite the heightening of the perceived level of threat engendered by the Camp David accords, the Syrians did not respond by increasing the size of either their regular army or their reserves between 1977 and 1981 (see table 1). Instead, most of the increased expenditures went toward upgrading and mechanizing the existing forces.

The stated Syrian goal in the years following Camp David was to achieve "strategic parity" with Israel. As Asad explained it, this parity was a necessary precondition to any just resolution of Syria's long-standing conflict with Israel — whether through war or through negotiation. More-over, as the prospects for an effective coalition with Iraq disappeared, Syrian spokesmen explained that this parity would have to be achieved by Syria on a one-to-one basis with Israel. The well-informed Asad biographer Patrick Seale has said that the Syrian president arrived at his view of strategic parity

> from his gloomy observation of the course of Sadat's peace diplomacy. In his view, Sadat had not made peace with Israel, he had capitulated: Sinai had not been liberated, Egypt itself had been fettered. Peace, he concluded, was not for the weak.[23]

As was the case in Israel, for Syrian decision makers, a relationship with a superpower was an important factor in assessing the nation's strategic situation. Syria had been heavily dependent on Soviet and Eastern bloc arms since the 1950s. In a 1987 interview, Foreign Minister Farouq al-Sharaa defined Syria's concept of its strategic balance with Israel as "the sum of the Israel-Syria balance plus the superpower commitments to both sides." Sharaa said that "if the superpowers have a balance in the region, they can impose a just peace. And then we wouldn't need strategic parity just for Syria." He added: "We are deeply concerned about the increase in Israeli-American strategic cooperation, especially under President Reagan. The U.S. administration thinks that its alliance with Israel can serve to impose peace on the Arabs [on its terms]."[24]

Relations between Syria and its superpower backer had never been free of tensions. On the important question

of the Arab-Israeli peace process, though both parties opposed American unilateralism in the region, the Soviets
never shared the goal, articulated by Syrian leaders in earlier years, of getting rid of "the Zionist entity" (Israel) completely.[25] Throughout the 1970s the Soviets had been pressing the Syrians to conclude a formal treaty with them.
Through 1978 Asad resisted the Soviet pressures for numerous reasons. Possibly, he assumed that it would be accompanied by a measure of unwelcome Soviet control. He
probably feared that it might constrain his already limited
ability to maneuver Syria's position between the two superpowers. Finally, Asad had to calculate the probable political fallout from a treaty. In Syria, his own Alawi Muslim
group made up only 12 percent of the national population
and felt constantly under threat from activists in the
majority Sunni Muslim community. A formal treaty with
the USSR would almost certainly alienate a further seg-
ment of observant Sunnis, upsetting the fragile internal
balance. Outside Syria, formalization of the link with the
Soviets might decrease the willingness of the anti-Soviet
Saudis and other Gulf Arabs to continue to bankroll Asad's
regime.

From late 1978 on, however, there were signs that the
pressures on Asad to accede to the Soviets' desire for the
treaty were becoming stronger. The final Syrian decision
to go ahead with a treaty came after the 1979 break with
Iraq and was most likely made in response to that development. In October 1979 Asad visited Moscow and concluded
the largest arms deal to date between the two countries,
which reportedly included the transfer to Syria over the
years ahead of some 1,400 tanks, 200 combat aircraft,
2,000 armored vehicles, and 1,700 artillery pieces. Contacts
between the sides intensified, and in October 1980 they
concluded a formal Treaty of Friendship and Cooperation.[26]

The treaty provided that if the security of either of
the parties were jeopardized, the two would "enter without
delay into contact with each other." The month after it was
signed, the Syrians sent a threatening group of tanks down

to their southern border with Jordan, awakening some fears that a repeat of Syria's 1970 intervention in Jordan would present the superpowers with a global political crisis. In 1980 the Syrian tank force never crossed the Jordanian border; it dispersed as quickly and mysteriously as it had gathered. The best explanation of this action is that it was intended primarily as a signal from Asad to internal opponents of the treaty with Moscow that the treaty had not curtailed his freedom to conduct Syria's national decision making. But the Syrian leader thereby sent his new treaty partner a defiant declaration of independence. For their part, the Soviets maintained a tight-lipped silence about the affair.[27]

Deterioration and Confrontation in Lebanon, 1981–1982

The Red Lines agreements regulating the interaction of Israel and Syria in Lebanon had survived the challenge posed to them by the 1978 Litani Operation, and they remained effective until April 1981. That month, the (Christian) Lebanese militias with whom the Israelis were working in central Lebanon were able to draw Israel into an action that challenged some of the basic tenets of the agreements: Israeli planes shot down two helicopters carrying Syrian troops on peacekeeping duties in the Bekaa Valley. An outraged Asad responded to this infringement of the agreements with one of his own: he deployed a number of surface-to-air missile (SAM) batteries to the area. Syria was thus left with precisely the air-defense capability in Lebanon that the agreements had sought to preclude.[28]

As the Israeli strategic analyst Yair Evron has pointed out, this development did not materially raise the level of threat against Israeli air actions in Lebanon, but it was construed by Prime Minister Menachem Begin (who at this stage was acting as his own defense minister) as a serious blow to the overall deterrent effect of the Red Lines agreements. He and his cabinet, therefore, voted on April 30 to take out the Syrian air-defense missile batteries with additional air strikes. Cloud cover prevented these strikes from taking place immediately, however, and by the time the clouds had cleared the Americans had had time to persuade Begin to pursue a diplomatic approach to "the Syrian missile crisis." Throughout the year that followed, U.S. special envoy Philip Habib tried unsuccessfully to find a negotiated formula for resolving the crisis. Although his attempt failed, his repeated shuttles between Israel and Syria provided an important channel between the two leaderships throughout that crucial period.

With a general election due within the coming months, Begin and his hard-line chief of staff, Rafael Eitan, turned their attention from the embarrassing stalemate over the Syrian missiles to raising the pressure against the Palestinians in Lebanon. At the end of May and again in July, Israel renewed its air and sea bombardments of PLO concentrations there. On the second of these occasions, the Israeli air force bombed targets in a heavily populated part of Beirut, leaving well over 200 dead.[29] Although they were well aware of the risks involved in escalation, the PLO leaders at this point abandoned their previous policy of restraint, and for two weeks they maintained a campaign of bombardments that, while it caused few Israeli casualties, forced many residents of Israel's northernmost communities to flee elsewhere for their safety.

Between these two rounds of Israeli-PLO fighting, the Israeli cabinet also launched its spectacularly successful raid against Iraq's nuclear reactor. With national security excitement thus running at fever pitch in Israel, Begin's Likud bloc came in first in the July 1981 elections. This time, Begin appointed as his defense minister a man who reportedly already harbored some hard-hitting plans for dealing with the situation in Lebanon — the ebullient former commander of Israel's southern front (and agriculture minister), Ariel Sharon. Sharon's appointment signaled a new era in Israeli national security decision making because he possessed little of the caution that had marked the advice that Begin—a man lacking personal military experience—had received from the military experts in his previous cabinet.[30]

In October 1981, the new Israeli government concluded an important, formal MOU on strategic collaboration with the United States. Barely two months later, Begin made an unexpected move by proposing and winning Knesset approval for a motion extending Israeli law to the Golan. That angered the Americans; the Reagan administration responded by abruptly suspending the strategic collaboration agreement. As for the Syrians, Ze'ev Schiff judged that they were correct when they "understood the Knesset resolution of approval, which was adopted by a 63–21 majority, to mean that Israel in effect had shut the door on negotiations for a peaceful settlement in return for Syrian territory."[31]

Habib was meanwhile continuing his shuttle diplomacy, although with little visible effect. Then on June 3, 1982, a Palestinian gunman shot and wounded the Israeli ambassador in London. The PLO immediately disavowed responsibility (and were later proved not to have been responsible), but the next day, the Israelis launched punishing air raids against PLO positions in Beirut and south Lebanon, killing at least 45. The PLO leaders responded by sending a few dozen artillery shells and rockets into northern Israel. By the time they landed, the IDF was already completing preparations for the massive invasion of Lebanon—the broad outlines of which had been planned throughout the previous months.

On June 6, the IDF Command sent six divisions into action in Lebanon. As Yair Evron and others have noted, the suppression of the PLO alone, which was the ostensible mission of the invasion, would have required no more than one or two divisions. Nor was there any effective Lebanese national army to confront. Evron was thus probably correct in concluding that the large size of the Israeli force indicated "that a military confrontation with Syria was

planned from the outset."[32] For their part, Ze'ev Schiff and
Ehud Ya'ari wrote that beginning in late 1981, Sharon was
talking to aides about the need to destroy the PLO, not
only in south Lebanon but also in Beirut; about installing,
during the elections scheduled for August in Lebanon, a
pro-Israeli government that would prevent the PLO from
returning to Beirut; and about the need to eliminate the
Syrians from Lebanon in the process.[33] Realizing these
broad political aims would necessarily involve sending a
sizable Israeli force all the way to Beirut.

On June 6, 1982, Sharon and Begin were still unwilling
to divulge the full extent of this "Big Plan" in Lebanon to
the Americans, the Israeli people, or even their own cabinet. Instead, while sending the six divisions required by
the Big Plan into southern Lebanon, they announced that
their objective was merely to remove the PLO and allied
forces from the area within 40 kilometers (25 miles) of Israel's border and that the Syrian army would not be attacked
"unless it attacks our forces."[34] Then they waited to gauge
the international reactions. Sharon's own expectation was
that "if the fighting was not inside Syria, the Soviets would
not intervene."[35] Neither on this score nor with respect to
the U.S. reaction would he be disappointed. The Soviet reaction was, as expected, fairly mild. And it soon became
clear to Sharon and Begin that U.S. President Ronald
Reagan and Secretary of State Haig had opted to back the
Israeli action, at least insofar as it was aimed at effecting
a pro-Western order in Lebanon. Evron wrote that these
reactions "created a context within which Begin decided
that the 'Big Plan' was in fact politically feasible."[36]

On June 8, as the Israeli divisions continued plowing
northward into Lebanon over three broad fronts, Begin met
with U.S. envoy Habib and asked him to communicate directly to Asad that "Israel did not wish to fight Syria,
and would not attack Syrian forces unless attacked first."
Habib left for Syria almost immediately. Before he went
into his meeting with Asad the following day, however, the
Israeli air force had launched the first of a series of ex-

tremely successful strikes against the Syrian SAMs in the Bekaa. The IDF had already, on June 8, launched a number of other attacks against Syrian positions south of Beirut that were well within the area in which Syrian ground forces deployments had been sanctioned by the Red Lines agreements.[37] Asad and Habib were thus placed in a somewhat difficult position during their meeting. Nevertheless, as Evron judged it, the Syrian leader "persisted in his attempt to limit the imminent escalation." Indeed, Evron wrote that in his response to Habib, Asad "demonstrated his readiness to acquiesce in the destruction of the PLO and in a very deep extension of Israeli forces in Lebanon. He also signalled his readiness to accept American mediation." But the Israeli writer noted that Asad also sent a strong signal about the location of Syria's Red Line: "Simultaneously, Syria began to move reinforcements to the Beqaa signalling its determination to defend its position there."[38]

Patrick Seale has written that, after the Israeli actions against the SAMs, "there was no . . . room for doubt in Asad's mind that Israel aimed to destroy him. Now the question for him was: Would Sharon's armies surge forward to the Beirut-Damascus road, cutting off Syrian forces in Beirut and the mountains, or would they turn east and threaten Damascus itself?" He added that "with vital security interests at stake Asad now had to stand and fight."[39] Over the two days that followed, Asad sent substantial reinforcements to strengthen the sub-division-level Syrian units in Lebanon. These reinforcements included two armored divisions which, along with Syrian commando battalions, acquitted themselves very creditably in the ground battle—particularly because they had no hope of any air cover. Asad also sent wave after wave of fighter-planes into Lebanon on what, given the destruction of the SAMs and Israel's considerable air superiority, were fore-doomed to be nothing more than suicide missions.[40]

It is also important to note, however, the deployment decisions that Asad refrained from making at this time.

He held Syria's other four major army divisions back from Lebanon. And though he had, on June 8, sent five new SAM-6 batteries into Lebanon, these came not from Damascus but from the Golan Heights, which clearly indicated to the Israelis that he was not planning to respond to the attacks inside Lebanon by opening up the Golan front.[41] Meanwhile, no preparations were reported for moving into Lebanon any of Syria's strategic-level air-defense batteries, such as the SAM-2s and SAM-3s, which remained in place defending the Syrian heartland.

The Americans meanwhile continued their efforts to get a cease-fire into place. On June 9, President Reagan sent a letter to Premier Begin in which he gave the following warning:

> I am extremely concerned by the latest reports of additional advances of Israel into central Lebanon and the escalation of violence between Israel and Syria. Your forces moved significantly beyond the objectives that you have described to me. . . .
>
> Today I received a letter from President Brezhnev which voices grave concern. . . .
>
> I now call on you to accept a ceasefire as of 6:00 A.M. on Thursday 10 June 1982. . . .
>
> Menachem, a refusal by Israel to accept a ceasefire will aggravate further the serious threat to world peace and will create extreme tension in our relations.[42]

Implementation of the cease-fire took 30 hours longer than Reagan had indicated in this letter, and it remained in effect only in the strategically critical eastern sector bordering Syria, while it quickly eroded in Lebanon's central mountains and in and around Beirut. According to Evron, the Israelis' decision to abide by it in the east was prompted primarily by U.S. insistence that they do so.[43]

As Seale revealed, President Asad took advantage of the breathing space provided by the June 11 cease-fire to fly secretly to the Soviet capital. There he prompted an ailing General-Secretary Leonid Brezhnev to contact President Reagan once again.[44] The subsequent judgments of those who were in the decision-making loop in Washington in 1982 were mixed on the extent to which the U.S. messages to Israel had been influenced by the Soviet factor. One U.S. participant classed the Soviet communications of this period as not particularly alarming, but hinted that the United States might have put its own "spin" on them when relaying them to the Israelis. Another said that he considered the Soviet communications more serious, especially because he reported that they were accompanied by the upgrading of the alert status of some Soviet airborne units in the southern USSR.[45]

Whatever the truth on that score, it does seem that from June 11 on the Israeli leaders understood that the U.S. injunction against continuing the fighting was particularly strong with respect to the eastern Lebanon (Bekaa Valley) front. Because they now judged that they could realize their goal of establishing a pro-Israeli government in Beirut without having to fight further in the east, they were unwilling to risk a major disagreement with the Americans over the situation there.[46] In later years, Sharon was to blame the Americans bitterly for having prevented him from cutting the Beirut-Damascus highway just where he wanted to—near Lebanon's border with Syria.[47] There is no evidence, however, that even this move would have shaken the self-control with which Asad held the bulk of his forces back from the Lebanese killing fields.

If Sharon were to ensure success in installing a friendly government in Beirut, however, the IDF still had to advance farther north in the central mountain sector overlooking the city in order to link up with the friendly Falangist militia in east Beirut and thus complete the encirclement of the PLO and allied forces in west Beirut. To achieve this, the IDF would have to punch through the positions that the Syrians were occupying in the mountain sector along and to the south of the Beirut-Damascus highway. The Israeli cabinet was by now fairly wary of further engagement with the Syrians (apart from those Syrian

forces trapped alongside the PLO in the punishing siege of
Beirut). But in the third week of the war, Begin went to
Washington. In his absence Sharon launched the attack
against the Syrian positions in the mountains and achieved
his objectives after a costly battle.[48] From their mountain-
top positions the Israelis were now in total strategic command of Beirut and its environs and, with the Falangists,
had thrown a tight noose around the PLO headquarters
forces in West Beirut. When the Lebanese parliamentari-
ans convened in August to elect their next president, they
did so under the protection of Israeli guns. The only candidate was the youthful Falangist militia boss, Bashir Gemayel. (In 1976 Gemayel's predecessor had been elected under the protection of Syrian guns.)

In the weeks between June and the election, the IDF
continued its pressure on the hundreds of thousands of
Lebanese and Palestinians trapped in West Beirut. (One
Syrian combat brigade was also trapped in Beirut. It
fought on, in coordination with the PLO command there.)
The Israelis soon realized that they would be unable to take
the city without incurring unacceptable casualties and that
the Falangists would not be following up on previous agreements to do the job for them. Therefore, in an attempt to
force the PLO out of the city, they relied on a combination
of a tight siege, heavy bombings, a barrage of psychologi-
cal warfare techniques – and negotiation.[49]

The negotiations were conducted through U.S. envoy
Habib. By the end of July, he had secured a PLO agreement to evacuate Beirut, but he still needed to find Arab
countries willing to take in the Palestinian forces. Asad
reportedly sensed that this was the last means of leverage
that he could use against the U.S. plan in Lebanon. So at
first he refused to cooperate in the evacuation plans; after
he saw the Israelis trying to force him to cooperate through
an unexpected bombardment of his forces in the Bekaa, he
dug in his heels even deeper.[50] By August 10, however,
Asad sensed that PLO Chairman Yasir Arafat had decided
to leave Beirut anyway. Asad decided that if Syria were to

retain any influence at all over the Palestinians, he had better allow them to leave through Syria.

The trapped Palestinian and Syrian forces evacuated Beirut during the last week of August.[51] But Syria was not totally shorn of leverage in Lebanon. On September 14, a Lebanese activist, believed to be acting on Syrian orders, planted a bomb in Bashir Gemayel's headquarters that ripped the building apart, killing Bashir along with 23 others, who were mainly Falangist functionaries. This event presented Sharon and Begin with an urgent dilemma. After all the losses that the IDF had sustained in Lebanon, and with all of the strains that the invasion had placed on Israel's domestic and international relations, was the Lebanese presidency now to slip out of their grasp? In an effort to prevent such a contingency, the Israeli cabinet decided on the night of September 14–15 to send the IDF into West Beirut. The deployment took place at dawn the next day.

Sharon and IDF Chief of Staff Eitan decided to take Falangist units with them into West Beirut to take control of the (now defenseless) Palestinian refugee camps. For 36 hours starting on the evening of September 16, while IDF units surrounded the camps and provided logistical support, the Falangists engaged in an orgy of killing that left many hundreds, possibly thousands, of camp residents dead and horribly mutilated.[52]

When television footage of this carnage reached world media markets on September 18, public opinion everywhere was rocked by revulsion at the Falangists' behavior. This presented the Israeli and U.S. governments with tough dilemmas. Sharon had promised the increasingly war-weary Israeli public that the IDF move into Beirut had been aimed at preserving calm. And the United States had guaranteed to Arafat both that the IDF would not move into Beirut after the PLO evacuation and that the safety of the remaining Palestinian noncombatants would be ensured.[53]

In Israel, huge demonstrations gathered in the streets protesting the massacre and calling for Sharon's ouster. In Washington, the president issued a curt demarche to the

Israelis to withdraw to their previous lines outside the city. Attempting to retrieve some of the badly eroded U.S. credibility, the administration arranged for the urgent return to Beirut of the U.S. Marines and the other components of the Multi-National Force (MNF) that, having successfully overseen the PLO's evacuation, had left Beirut two weeks before. With little ado, the Lebanese deputies met again. They elected as president Bashir's elder brother, Amin Gemayel, through whom Sharon now sought to consolidate his gains in Lebanon.

Syria's Post-1982 Offensive in Lebanon

From the moment of Bashir Gemayel's assassination, the Syrians seized the initiative in the Lebanese arena. The continuation of Israel's overall strategic superiority over Syria meant that the resurgence of Syrian power in Lebanon could not be generalized from there to the overall strategic equation. But Syria's return to a position of influence in Lebanon and its ability to regain the ground-level predominance there that it had lost in 1982 enabled Asad to remain in power and his regime to remain an important player in the Middle Eastern regional game. It also resulted in policy achievements that the Soviets considered important and thus for a number of years ensured a greater degree of Soviet support for Asad's regime than would otherwise have been the case.

The victories that Asad registered in Lebanon between 1982 and 1985 resulted primarily from the mistakes made there by his enemies—the United States, Israel, and the Falangists. Indeed, it can be argued that if the United States had used its influence to urge President Gemayel toward internal political reform and the Israelis toward a speedy withdrawal, then a fairly durable pro-U.S. regime might have been installed in Beirut, leaving Syria on the sidelines. The United States, however, adopted no such policy. It indulged the preference of Gemayel's Falangist

Party to abstain from addressing the issue of internal reform. And, far from pressing for an Israeli withdrawal, successive U.S. envoys came increasingly to view Israel's continued presence in south Lebanon as far as the outskirts of
Beirut as helpful leverage against the Syrians. When the
Israelis' own deep war-weariness and internal divisions led
them in September 1983 to withdraw unilaterally from the
Shouf region, the United States actually urged that they
postpone the move.

As for the Israeli leaders, their mistakes in Lebanon
were also serious. Their first mistake, dating back to the
early days of the June 1982 invasion, was to plan the action
on the basis of Falangist promises of cooperation that the
Falangists proved unable and unwilling to keep. A more
serious mistake was that implementation of the Big Plan
in Lebanon stretched Israel's crucial national security consensus nearly to the breaking point. From June 1982 on,
the Israeli public made increasingly clear that it did not
consider the (dubious) achievements of the Big Plan worth
all of the human losses and moral opprobrium that their
country had incurred in implementing it. The Lebanon war
has rightly been described by many in Israel as "Israel's
Vietnam."

Syria's achievements in Lebanon from 1982 to 1985,
however, were not only the result of its foes' mistakes. They
also reflected the steady hand and cool strategic judgment
of President Asad. As Patrick Seale reported it, Asad's
first priorities as the newly churned mud hardened on the
Lebanese battlefields were "to encourage guerrilla harass-
ment of Israel in Lebanon, while racing to rebuild Syria's
own armed strength."[54] The Syrian leader proved remarkably successful in the first of these endeavors and fairly
successful in the second—at a stage in his career during
which he also had to cope with a debilitating bout of ill
health and the emergence of a bitterly divisive, if prema-
ture, succession struggle in Damascus.

Harassing Israel's extended presence in Lebanon
proved relatively easy for Asad. The Syrian presence that

had been maintained in Lebanon between 1976 and 1982 had often aroused the deep resistance of the locals; in June 1982 the IDF received what it considered a gratifyingly warm welcome in many south Lebanese villages. The most basic instinct, however, of Lebanese of all sects has always been to resent any prolonged foreign occupation. And for many Lebanese, it soon seemed that the IDF, too, was outstaying its welcome. Moreover, in the case of that large majority of Lebanese who opposed the Falangists' domination of their government, Israel's many continuing links with the Falangists only further fueled the growing resentment against the IDF presence.[55]

Manipulating Lebanon's many internal schisms and rivalries was a game that the Syrians had been playing for decades. It was a game in which they enjoyed a comparative advantage over the less knowledgeable Israelis. It was also a game in which Syria's interests—both political and military, but especially the core interest of regime survival—were an entire order stronger than those of Israel.[56]

The results of Syria's support for the Lebanese dissidents were not long in coming. The Syrians found many ways to channel arms and money to activists operating behind Israeli lines, many of whom retained their proven clan and political networks intact. Actions against IDF positions multiplied in Beirut and in south Lebanon. The most spectacular of these came in November 1983, when a truck-bomb blew up the IDF staff headquarters in Tyre, killing 67. Asad had calculated that the continuation of human losses would weaken the Israelis' resolve in Lebanon, so he aimed to keep those losses high. According to a report published in an official IDF publication, between June 5, 1982 and May 31, 1985, 1,116 Israeli soldiers lost their lives in Lebanon—the majority of them after the PLO left Beirut.[57] In September 1983, the IDF unilaterally withdrew from the Shouf mountain area overlooking Beirut. This sent a strong signal that Israel was tiring of the struggle to retain its influence over the government there. Asad's strategy was already working.

While acting in Lebanon to push the Israelis back to their pre-1982 lines, Asad and his local allies also sought to diminish the influence of Gemayel's remaining foreign backer—the United States. The most obvious incarnation of the U.S. presence in Lebanon from September 1982 was the Marine-led Multi-National Force-2 (MNF-2), which was deployed principally around the airport south of Beirut. Unlike the first multilateral force, this force never had a clearly defined mission in Lebanon. It had been deployed in September 1982 as an immediate political response to the horrors of the Sabra and Shatila killings and stayed on with an ill-defined and ever-shifting mission of "presence" rather than combat.[58] This might have been feasible. In 1958, after all, an earlier Marine "presence" mission in Lebanon had successfully buttressed U.S. diplomacy there. On that earlier occasion, U.S. diplomats were quickly able to resolve the rampant local hostilities; the Marines then immediately left—having suffered only one casualty.[59] In the 1982–1984 period, by contrast, U.S. diplomacy paid scant attention to intra-Lebanese reconciliation. And as the intra-Lebanese hostilities grew fiercer beginning in early 1983, they swirled ever closer to the Marine encampment. Meanwhile, with U.S. military personnel separately out and about in Lebanon advising President Gemayel's national army as it battled Druze and other dissidents, it was not surprising that the dissidents also started taking action against the MNF-2 Marines.

The situation around the Marine camp became increasingly tense beginning in midsummer 1983. On October 23, 1983, two Lebanese Shi'a drove devastatingly effective truck-bombs into the barracks of the American and French MNF-2 contingents. The Marines lost 241 dead, and the French lost 57. (Seventeen Americans had been killed in April 1983 in a Shi'a bombing of the U.S. embassy in Beirut.) In Washington, Pentagon planners had always worried about the fuzzy nature of the MNF-2 mission, and by October the president was starting to prepare for the upcoming reelection campaign. After the October attack, the administration started serious internal discussions about how to remove the Marines from Beirut.

In the tangled mess of local and outside forces that constituted Lebanon, and in Syria itself, the pace of events meanwhile was quickening. On November 12, President Asad entered the hospital with a suspected heart complaint, for which his doctors prescribed a heavy dose of sedatives. He was indisposed for the next six weeks. With the president incapacitated, his powerful younger brother Rif'at al-Asad launched a challenge to his rule that would bring bitter divisions to Syria's multilayered army and security forces over the weeks ahead, until it was finally resolved in the president's favor in a dramatic face-to-face showdown at the end of March 1984.[60] Patrick Seale, whose account draws heavily on interviews with Asad himself, wrote that while Asad was sick, "his greatest worry was the war for Lebanon. While under treatment he had neglected to keep up with domestic affairs, but he had insisted on following the Lebanese crisis by telephone hour by hour."[61]

During the last weeks of 1983 in Lebanon, Syrian positions in the Bekaa were subjected to Israeli bombing raids, launched in reprisal for the Tyre truck-bomb attack; other Syrian units were meanwhile locked in a bloody fight to the finish with the PLO forces that had regrouped in the northern port city of Tripoli; and Syrian allies were engaged in increasingly direct confrontation with the U.S. presence in Beirut, while they openly battled the U.S.-backed Lebanese army in the mountains behind the capital. On December 4, four U.S. Navy fighter-bombers operating from the nearby Sixth Fleet carrier tried to attack Syrian air-defense batteries in the Bekaa Valley. On this occasion (in contrast to the Israeli performance the year before), two of the attacking planes were shot down, and one of the pilots was taken prisoner. During the three months that followed, the Sixth Fleet mounted intermittent naval bombardments against Syrian positions in Lebanon. According to Geoffrey Kemp, who was a Middle East specialist on

the National Security Council staff at the time, the rules
of engagement for the U.S. Navy forces in the area had
now been changed, and "the net effect was to support the
Lebanese army."[62] By now, this also meant engaging the
Syrians.

The continuing debate in Washington was given a last
sharp jolt on February 6, 1984, when most members of the
Lebanese army's predominantly Shi'ite 6th brigade de-
serted their posts en masse when faced with orders to fire
on coreligionists in south Beirut. Gemayel's authority col-
lapsed throughout south and west Beirut: the Marines now
found their encampment surrounded by the potentially
hostile Shi'ite militias. The following day, Reagan announced that he had decided to "re-deploy the Marines off-
shore" – that is, to withdraw them. According to Kemp, in
the Lebanese arena, "the U.S. Congress and the Pentagon
were not prepared to outwait the Syrians and increase military pressure to the point where Syria would withdraw its
forces."[63] As for the Syrian leader, Patrick Seale wrote that
Asad

> was somewhat incredulous that the United States had
> given up so easily. He told another Arab ruler: "The
> Americans are like children. When we opposed their
> policy in Lebanon, they launched one or two raids
> against us. We fired in the air and, lo and behold, two
> of their planes were shot down. So they pulled out!
> Well, let them go!"[64]

The announcement of MNF-2's withdrawal was welcomed by the Lebanese dissidents, by the Syrians, and by
the Soviets, who had seen the MNF-2 presence as another
link in the Pentagon's global counter-Soviet strategic planning (see chapter 4). At the end of the month, Gemayel
made his first state visit to Damascus, where he made
peace with a new protector – President Asad. The main condition Asad imposed on him was that Lebanon should abro-
gate the peace agreement with Israel that had been bro-

kered by the United States the previous May. Eager to retain the Lebanese presidency, Gemayel was more than willing to oblige.

The IDF still remained in place in broad areas of south Lebanon. But its casualty toll continued to rise, which rendered its position there increasingly untenable. In July 1985 a weary Israeli public applauded when the IDF was pulled back to virtually the same "security zone" that it had occupied prior to June 1982. Asad's strategy in Lebanon had triumphed.

In the years following 1985, as in the period before 1982, the Syrian leader would face enormous problems in achieving his political aims in Lebanon. To a large extent, however, once the Israelis and Americans had been expelled from Beirut and the primacy of his own influence was well established there, the details of a Lebanese settlement were a sideshow for Asad. With the Israeli threat removed from the Bekaa, he was able to withdraw some of his own ground forces from Lebanon and return them to Syria to retrain and to strengthen the Golan front. By July 1987 the Syrian deployment in Lebanon was reduced to an estimated 12,500 men. It did not begin to increase again until 1988 and then reached a figure estimated at 30,000 by July 1989.[65] On that occasion, however, the Syrians were responding to a Lebanon-centered challenge launched primarily by the Iraqis, not the Israelis. It remained unclear how long it would take this time to reach a situation in Lebanon that would enable them to scale back deployment.

Syria's Post-1982 Situation: The Force Buildup

Asad was able to orchestrate the Lebanese part of his post-1982 campaign with the help of only preexisting local forces. The other part, improving Syria's overall strategic capability, required substantial help from outside—principally from the Soviet Union.

Syria's armed forces were by no means completely destroyed in the 1982 encounter. Nevertheless, the helplessness that Asad felt that year proved a powerful incentive for a buildup of Syrian military strength. Just as Israeli strategic planning in the years following 1973 had been dominated by the need not to have to confront again the dilemmas of October 1973, so now, in the post-1982 period, Syrian planning was dominated by the need not to confront again the dilemmas of June 1982.

The first order of business was to regain some credible deterrent effect for Syria's air-defense capability. Syria already had a fairly dense air-defense system in 1982, including a number of "strategic," high-altitude systems (SAM-2s and SAM-3s) that were not directly engaged in the fighting in Lebanon. But the ease with which the IDF was able to suppress those SAM systems that were present in Lebanon, and the superior C^3I capabilities they revealed through their use of the Hawkeye and other airborne command and control systems, sent Asad running to Moscow for help. Seale recounts in a telling passage:

> To grab the Kremlin's attention, Asad argued that the United States was planning to use Israel and Lebanon as a springboard for further expansion, a thesis which seemed borne out by Reagan's decision in August 1982 to send US marines to Beirut. He [Asad] knew it would be to his advantage if the Soviet authorities saw the Middle East as a decisive prize in East-West competition.[66]

The Soviets were also worried by the capabilities that the Israelis had revealed in June 1982 — some of which were similar to those they themselves might have to face in a conventional confrontation in Europe. On June 13, 1982, the deputy commander-in-chief of the Soviet Air Defense Forces conducted an on-site inspection of the shattered Syrian SAM sites, and a month later Soviet Chief of Staff Nikolai Ogarkov followed him to Damascus.[67] Asad's big opportunity to elicit Soviet support, however, came in November 1982, when he visited Moscow to attend Brezhnev's funeral. There, he was able to renew his acquaintance with Brezhnev's successor, Yuri Andropov, whom he had first met during the secret trip to Moscow five months earlier. Asad and Defense Minister Mustafa Tlas, who accompanied him, were pleased at the hearing Andropov gave them—indeed, five years later, after two more successions in Moscow, Tlas was still lamenting the passing of Andropov.[68]

In January 1983 the strength of the Soviets' new commitment to Asad was demonstrated in dramatic fashion when it emerged that they had deployed a number of long-range SAM-5 air-defense missiles to Syria. This system had first entered the Soviet order of battle in the 1960s but had never been used in combat against Western forces. Western analysts estimated its range as relatively long, at about 185 miles (300 kilometers). It was widely thought in the West that a prime mission for the Syrian SAM-5s in any future Syrian-Israeli encounter would be to neutralize Israel's Hawkeyes, thus blinding the command and control component of much of Israel's air force.[69]

As is indicated by table 2, the strategic air defense component of the Syrian force structure was the first to have its strength increased after 1982. Between July 1982 and July 1983, the number of troops assigned to the Air Defense Command doubled from 20,000 to 40,000; and over the two years after that, as trained Syrians started taking over from the Soviets who at first manned the SAM-5s, this number further increased to 60,000.

Between 1982 and 1983, Syria continued to receive additional T-72 tanks from the Soviets, but these did not immediately result in an increase in the ground forces' order of battle, which remained stable between 1982 and 1983. Over the next four years, however, the ground forces increased their strength significantly—from six divisions that each comprised three brigades, plus six extra independent conventional brigades, in 1983, to nine divisions that each comprised five brigades in 1987. The special forces (parachute and commando) regiments that had, along with the armored units, performed creditably in 1982, were meanwhile organized into a special forces division comprising nine brigades. Four additional artillery brigades were meanwhile organized. (Three of these were later among those additional forces that were integrated into division-level operations, leaving three to operate independently.) Between 1983 and 1984, an additional surface-to-surface missile (SSM) regiment was also organized.

This regiment was armed with the SS-21s, which were, along with the SAM-5s, the most strategically sensitive items supplied to Syria by the Soviets in this period. The SS-21s, with their potential for striking with some accuracy at IDF mobilization centers or C^3I facilities, strengthened Syria's posture of general deterrence against Israel. According to the verdict reached in the 1986 edition of the annual review published by Tel Aviv University's Jaffee Center for Strategic Studies, "the Syrians now possess a weapons system . . . that, in contrast to the past, is capable of deterring Israel from initiating or even responding militarily against Syria's rear."[70] A more nuanced assessment would be that Syria had raised the threshold at which Israel would consider an attack against the Syrian rear to be a justifiable option.

By comparison with their air defense and ground forces, the Syrians' naval and air forces were not strengthened so strikingly in the years after 1982. In late 1985 the Syrians added to their strategic defenses the SS-C-1B (Sepal) coastal defense missile, whose long range might also allow them some offensive capability in the naval arena. Between 1982 and 1987, they added the following items to their naval order of battle: three R-class submarines, six Osa-II missile boats, seven patrol craft, six minesweepers, and 20 Mi-14 ASW helicopters.[71] These items would not, however, appear to give them anything approaching a trustworthy offensive capability against Israel's naval forces.

In that same period, the air force acquired 28 Su-17 fighter-ground-attack planes; 50 additional MiG-23s, in-

TABLE 2
Syrian Military Buildup after 1982:
Ground and Strategic Air Defense Forces

	1981	1982	1983	1984	1985	1986	1987
Armored divisions	4	4	4	4	5[a]	5[b]	5
Mechanized divisions	2	2	2	4	3[a]	3	4
Special forces divisions	0	0	0	n.a.	1[h]	1	1
Independent armored/ mechanized/infantry brigades	6	6	6	7	8	6	0?
Artillery brigades	2	2	2	5	6	3	3
Special forces regiments	6	6	6	9	8[h]	?	7
Surface-to-surface missile regimens	2	2	2	3[c]	3	3	3
Coastal defense brigades	0	0	0	0	0	1[d]	2[e]
Total tanks	3,700	3,990	4,200	4,100	4,200	4,200[f]	4,000
T-72/-72M	400	790	900	1,100	1,100	1,100	1,100

54

Strategic Air Defense (AD Command)

Batteries with SAM-2 and SAM-3	50	50	54	63	28	c.60	c.60
Batteries with SAM-6	25	25	25	31	27	27	27
Batteries with SAM-5	0	0	8[g]	8	8	8?	8?
Manpower (thousands)	20	20	40	50	60	60	c.60

[a]Strengthened by one additional armed brigade each.

[b]Further strengthened by one additional artillery brigade each.

[c]One regiment now with SS-21s.

[d]With SS-C-1B Sepal.

[e]One with SS-C-3.

[f]All estimated to be static antitank or reserve except 2,800.

[g]Four Soviet-manned sites.

[h]These two entries in the 1985 column may represent some double counting.

Source: The Military Balance for various years.

cluding some MiG-23Gs; six MiG-25R reconnaissance planes; and the relatively advanced AA-6 and AA-7 air-combat missiles.[72] But the two planes that the Syrians reportedly really wanted from the Soviets were the MiG-29, which they had reportedly been promised for quite some time before 1987, and the Su-24. The first delivery of 15 MiG-29s did not occur until midsummer 1987; and the second MiG-29 delivery was then similarly delayed. In 1989 the Soviets reportedly finally agreed to let the Syrians have some Su-24s.[73]

Syria's post-1982 military buildup reached a high point toward the end of 1986. According to informed Western sources, that year saw a number of corps-level maneuvers that provided an effective test of the ground forces' newly acquired capabilities.[74] No such maneuvers were held in the first half of 1987, however; by that point, two factors were acting to restrict any further buildup.

The first of these was a tightening resource crunch in both finances and capable manpower. The Syrian civilian economy was suffering evident damage in this period, caused by the diversion of resources to the military and by the ricochet effect from collapsing oil prices.[75] In terms of manpower, the scale of the military buildup at the high-technology end of the scale nearly drained the pool of available Syrian engineers and technicians, which then had a strangling effect on the civilian economy. Toward the end of 1986, the General Staff initiated a process of reductions in some of the ground forces. Some units in each of the large ground forces divisions were now cut back; the surplus manpower was transferred to the reserves, and the surplus equipment was mothballed.[76]

The Soviet constraint was potentially more crippling than the resource constraints because there was little that the regime itself could do to overcome it. Patrick Seale wrote of the post-1982 period:

> To secure the weapons and protection he needed Asad had to surrender a certain freedom of action. While he

retained control over tactical and operational matters, he lost some control over ultimate strategy. His aspiration for parity with Israel had become a Soviet benefaction, to give or to withhold. Moreover, with air defences and long-range missiles dependent on Soviet personnel, Syria could no longer consider starting hostilities as it had done in 1973; this too would have to be a Soviet decision.[77]

Seale was correct to pinpoint the increased dependency on Moscow that came with the mid-1980s arms shipments to Syria. But it would be wrong to conclude that, at the end of the 1980s, Asad had lost an ability to make a unilateral war decision that had existed prior to the mid-1980s buildup. Both before and after the buildup, such a decision carried a high risk of provoking a devastating Israeli counterpunch; therefore, any Syrian war decision would have to consider the chances that, either before or after the start of the war, the Soviets could be drawn in to help protect Syria's vital strategic installations – whether militarily or through diplomatic means. The fact that the Soviets might be keeping their fingers on the triggers of Syria's most powerful weapons, the SSMs, need not prevent Syria's leader from initiating a war without prior Soviet approval, if he considered it advisable to do so – for example, to revive the long-frozen negotiations over the Golan.[78] In the earlier case of Egypt, the fact that that country's SCUD missiles were still under Soviet control in 1973 did not prevent Sadat from deciding to go to war.[79] Asad might thus still calculate (as he and Sadat presumably had in 1973) that he could start a war on his own, so long as he could expect that once it started the Soviets would necessarily have to back him.

The signals Asad was receiving from the Soviets in 1987 and 1988 cannot have been encouraging for him. In April 1987, amid the pomp and publicity of a full state dinner in Moscow, General-Secretary Gorbachev openly lectured the Syrian president: "The stake on military power in settling the [Arab-Israeli] conflict has become completely discredited." Gorbachev also warned Asad that the absence of diplomatic relations between the Soviet Union and Israel "cannot be considered normal." And he disarmingly commended his guest for "the fact that Syrian leadership is unswervingly following the course toward a political settlement."[80] With Syrian public rhetoric in this period still stressing the need for "strategic parity" with Israel, Gorbachev's "fact" would seem to have been less than incontrovertible. Rather, the Soviet leader seemed to be setting a stern and public standard to which he hoped his dinner guest would adhere.

Israel's Situation, 1982–1989

The 1982 war was deeply traumatic for the Israelis. It rapidly became clear that the actual war aims of Sharon and Begin were far more ambitious than the aim the cabinet and public originally supported—that is, clearing out the PLO positions from the 40-kilometer strip north of the border. Achieving the broader aims, moreover, required that the IDF prevail in types of fighting for which it was ill-suited—primarily urban warfare. Thus, as it became clear that achieving Sharon's war aims would be neither quick nor easy and would involve a far higher level of Israeli casualties than Sharon had implied, worrying cracks appeared in a national security consensus that had held together during all of Israel's previous wars, even when mistakes had clearly been made.

The seriousness of the dissent was made public as early as the beginning of July 1982, when Colonel Eli Geva, one of the IDF's most talented tank commanders, resigned rather than carry out orders to attack Lebanese civilians in Beirut.[81] The trauma over the war then deepened further in the aftermath of the Sabra and Shatila massacres. In response to the public outcry provoked in Israel by the massacres, the Begin government appointed a blue-ribbon commission under Judge Yitzhak Kahan to investigate the involvement of Israeli officials in the affair. The commission's report was issued in February 1983. It found that Foreign Minister Yitzhak Shamir and several of the IDF's top commanders all bore some indirect responsibility for what had happened, primarily through sins of omission rather than commission. It arrived at "grave conclusions" concerning the actions of chief of staff Rafael Eitan. But Eitan was about to resign his post, so the commission made no further recommendation in his case. The brunt of the report's opprobrium was reserved for Sharon. It said that he bore "personal responsibility" for what had happened in the camps.[82]

The commission recommended that Sharon "draw the appropriate conclusions"—that is, resign. Sharon tried to resist, but mounting public pressure soon forced his hand. Even then, however, Begin kept him in the cabinet without portfolio.[83]

Throughout the years that followed 1982, Sharon continued to defend the achievements of the war that he had been primarily responsible for planning and executing. In May 1985, for example, he listed these achievements in the following terms:

- The PLO was eliminated as a major political and military element. . . . The defeat of the PLO engendered the most positive effect in Judaea, Samaria [the West Bank] and the Gaza Strip. . . .
- Our deployment deep into Lebanon and on the flank of the Damascus plain in effect destroyed the Syrians' ability to attack us on the Golan as well. . . .
- Israel's "preventive interdiction" jumped several stages ahead in one fell swoop. . . .
- Our real political and strategic situation . . . has improved immeasurably.[84]

Sharon's critics, both inside and outside the uniformed military, challenged these conclusions. As early as September 1982, Military Intelligence chief Yehoshua Saguy judged that "the Syrians have not been substantially weakened militarily. . . . If we talk about numbers, equipment and weapons, the Syrians have not been defeated. Moreover, they have been strengthened."[85]

Military historian Martin Van Creveld had a more damning indictment:

> By 1982 the IDF was, relative to its size, as well armed as any force the world has ever seen. . . .
>
> In Lebanon, this combination of quantity with technological sophistication made it possible to avoid any kind of military thought. . . . The IDF in Lebanon piled tank upon tank and gun upon gun.
>
> A command and control system superior to anything previously employed made it possible to achieve good interarm cooperation and, above all, spew forth vast amounts of ammunition to destroy the country which the IDF had allegedly come to save.
>
> The results, nevertheless, were disappointing. The traditional superiority of individual Israeli troops and crews over their opponents took a nosedive.[86]

The following year, intelligence veteran Zvi Lanir wrote:

> The utilization of the army in the Lebanese war was marked by an excess of force and overwhelming superiority in firepower. The enemy was to a certain extent outgunned rather than outmaneuvered, pounded into submission instead of being outflanked, and crushed by siege instead of being overwhelmed by a war of movement. . . .
>
> But in the final analysis, the basic contradiction of the war stemmed from the attempt to achieve Clausewitzian goals through the utilization of a military machine trained and indoctrinated to attain a decisive victory. . . . In the end, this threatened the attainment of the Clausewitzian goals themselves.[87]

As happened with many other Israeli strategic thinkers, Lanir sought in the post-Lebanon period to reexamine
some of the deepest foundations of Israeli doctrine. "Israeli
doctrine is in crisis," he stated in an interview in July 1987.
"The state has had no clearly defined war aims in any of its
wars since 1956."[88]

Not only fundamental issues of doctrine but some of
the most hallowed tenets of Israeli strategy and operational art came in for criticism in this period.[89] And there
were numerous discussions of the financial costs of maintaining Israel's huge defense establishment—especially
with its heavily inflated deployment in Lebanon, which
sapped the Israeli economy both by increasing reservists'
service obligations and by fueling a punishing spiral of
price inflation at home.[90]

While the Israelis were in the midst of these debates in
late summer and autumn of 1983, two momentous events
occurred. In September 1983, Premier Begin withdrew
from public life; his place at the head of the Likud Party
and the government was taken by Yitzhak Shamir. Then,
two months later, the Reagan administration formally res-
urrected the strategic collaboration with Israel that had
lain dormant since December 1981, which ended the strain
in the relationship that had begun with the refugee camp
massacres.

In a speech honoring Shamir at the end of November
1983, Reagan explained that the joint political-military
group (JPMG) established by the new collaboration agreement would "give priority attention to the threat to our
mutual interests posed by increased Soviet involvement in
the Middle East."[91] It would also, over the years ahead,
provide a channel through which the Israeli defense establishment could gain access to large amounts of American
defense goods, up to a new high point on the technological
spectrum. The agreement would thus have its own effect
on the strategic debate within Israel in the second half of
the 1980s (see chapter 3).

In 1983, the parts of the Israeli strategic debate that

had a perceptible impact on policy were the twin issues of
the value of the war's aims in Lebanon and the costs involved in keeping the IDF there. As noted above, by the
summer of 1983, the government was already reconsider-
ing the value of keeping troops stationed in the Beirut area;
in September it ordered the unilateral withdrawal from the
Shouf region. Even after this partial pullback, however, the
debate still continued over maintaining the rest of the
IDF's presence in Lebanon.

In summer 1984, as the end of Likud's four-year term
in office drew near, Shamir called an election. The voting
resulted in a near tie between Likud and Labor. After ex-
tensive haggling, the two parties agreed on a unique "national unity government" formula, under which they would
rotate the posts of premier and foreign minister between
them, with Labor's Shimon Peres taking first turn in the
premier's seat. The coalition agreement stipulated both a
withdrawal from Lebanon and measures to regain control
of the national economy.

The costs of maintaining the IDF's extended presence
in Lebanon had already been huge, in terms of both human
life and finances. In March 1985 the Israeli treasury was
reported to have allocated a total of approximately $1.3
billion to finance the war effort in Lebanon over the preceding three years.[92] The cost of the engagement there had
thus averaged more than $1 million a day for Israel. In
fall 1982 the U.S. Congress had voted to increase the aid
allocation to Israel by $475 million. Although that alloca-
tion went far toward meeting the immediate costs of the
invasion of Lebanon, it also further fueled the inflationary
process that had already been a serious problem in Israel
before 1982 and continued to be compounded so long as a
significant part of government spending was poured into
the large troop presence in Lebanon. Thus, while inflation
ran at 101.5 percent in 1981, in 1982 it increased to 120.4
percent, rising to a high point of 373 percent in 1984.[93]

In 1985 the national unity government set to work on
its two, closely related, main tasks — economic reform and

the withdrawal from Lebanon. Inflation that year was pulled back to 185 percent through a combination of belt-tightening, economic reforms, and withdrawal from Lebanon. (The next year, inflation was down to a manageable 25 percent.) By July 1985 the IDF had returned to virtually the same "security zone" in south Lebanon from which it had launched its offensive three years earlier.

In the context of Israel's budgetary squeeze of the mid-1980s, the local-currency defense budget came under scrutiny along with all other government spending, although the defense budget cuts were less severe than those for most nondefense items. Although the level of defense expenditures based on local resources had totaled about $3.2 billion in 1982, by 1986 the sum allocated to local expenditures came to only $2.54 billion. This reduction in the local-currency budget was partly mitigated by an increase in the annual level of U.S. defense aid, from $1.4 billion to $1.8 billion, that came into effect in 1986.[94] In contrast to the prevailing situation for most recipients of U.S. aid, the aid dollars came to be viewed within the Israeli defense establishment in this period as relatively "soft" money; defense planners thus tried to convert as many transactions as possible into the dollar economy.[95]

The budgetary situation mandated real cuts in those expenditures, principally manpower expenses, that could not easily be thus converted. Thus, the number of Israelis in the standing army was cut by 19 percent between 1982 and 1987—from 174,000 to 141,000. (A proportion of those cut from the standing force were transferred to the reserve, whose numbers reportedly increased from 326,000 to 504,000 over the same period. See table 1.) By trimming off excess administrative "tail" from combat units and transferring some of the ground forces divisions to skeleton status, the paper order of battle was retained at roughly its pre-Lebanon level (see table 3). Thus, from 1982 through 1987, the IDF retained 11 armored divisions. The number of independent mechanized infantry brigades dropped from 10 to 9. But the new stress on mountain and urban warfare

TABLE 3
Israeli Order of Battle (Selected Items), 1982 and 1987

Service	1982	1987
Army		
Armored divisions	11	11[a]
Mechanized infantry brigades	10	9
Infantry brigades	0	3
Paratroop brigades	0	5
Artillery brigades	15	15
Air defense batteries	2	2
Tanks	3,600	3,900
Air Force		
Combat aircraft	634	676
	(270 stored?)	(90 stored?)
Attack helicopters	42	76

[a]Many cadre.
Source: The Military Balance, 1982–1983 and 1987–1988.

that resulted from the experiences in Lebanon led to the establishment of a total of 8 paratroop and nonmechanized infantry brigades in that same period.[96]

Other activities affected by the mid-1980s budget squeeze included training of reserve formations, investments in logistics, and procurement. In this last area, Israeli analysts calculated that between 1984 and 1985, IDF procurement from local military industries declined over 40 percent, leading to the closing of a number of production lines and the dismissal of thousands of technicians from the weapons plants affected.[97]

The major procurement decision for the government in the mid-1980s was whether to proceed with the development of Israel's own next-generation fighter plane, the Lavi, or to buy upgraded F-16s from the United States.[98] By 1986 it was clear to most of the IDF high command, including the air force commanders, that the Lavi project would ultimately consume a disproportionate amount of the IDF's future procurement budgets, while its repeated delays threatened to leave Israel without a new-generation plane for the early 1990s. In July 1987 Defense Minister Yitzhak Rabin obtained terms from the United States under which, in return for canceling the Lavi project, Israel would be given F-16-Cs and -Ds additional to those already programmed for delivery, and still get $300 million of defense aid per year to spend in the local economy. The government soon agreed to this package, which promised to be far cheaper and more effective than proceeding with the Lavi.[99]

Another large-scale procurement decision that faced the IDF concerned the navy's desire for three new diesel-powered submarines and four new missile-boats. The major problem here was that the United States no longer built diesel-powered submarines, and there was a question of whether U.S. defense aid could be spent on acquiring these for Israel from West Germany. By early 1988 this had been agreed to, though with one less vessel in each class than the navy had hoped for, and the naval procurement program was finally under way.[100]

As table 3 shows, the IDF's inventories of matériel were not substantially increased in most other categories in the post-Lebanon period. One exception was attack helicopters, whose effectiveness had been demonstrated in the 1982 fighting. But the inventories continued to be upgraded.[101]

Meanwhile, the IDF's all-important human component was facing some worrying issues. IDF officers and soldiers were facing belt-tightening and large-scale layoffs at the same time that they were integrally caught up in the entire post-Lebanon debate over the purpose and utility of Israeli military might. In November 1985, for example, the head of the IDF manpower branch admitted that the pay of army regulars had been eroded by between 15 and 18 percent in real terms over the previous two years and that some of them were now approaching the poverty line.[102]

In August 1985 Ze'ev Schiff published a series of articles charting the decline in IDF morale. He judged that "the undermining of the IDF's self-image has been an ongoing process. The turning-point apparently came following the Yom Kippur war [of 1973], but the Lebanon war accelerated the growth of this negative image." Schiff identified increasing problems in the area of discipline, writing that "the latter part of the war in Lebanon brought the situation to a new nadir."[103] In March 1986 one of Schiff's colleagues agonized over the general erosion in the IDF's operational norms: "Soldiers are trained in an atmosphere in which in many cases the desire 'not to get involved' becomes the main thing."[104]

The IDF command recognized the gravity of these morale problems, and once the withdrawal back to the Lebanese "security zone" had been completed, it started to address them. Approximately 30 months after the withdrawal, however, widespread troop morale problems were still being pinpointed in press analyses of the "hang glider affair" of November 1987, in which a Palestinian guerrilla managed to breach Israel's northern defenses in a hang glider, landing near an army camp where, amidst the confusion of the camp guards, he was able to kill six soldiers before he himself was killed.[105] Shortly after that debacle, the IDF's human component was faced with a totally new kind of challenge in the form of the Palestinian civilian uprising (*intifada*) in the West Bank and Gaza.

The *intifada* posed a challenge, as did the Lebanese engagement before it, at the levels of troop morale and manpower planning. Concerning morale, the need to use troops to suppress repeated civilian riots raised questions relating to the long-standing IDF norm of "purity of arms."[106] Meanwhile, the IDF command was forced to increase the annual reserve commitment from 30 days to a high point of 62 days, in circumstances in which senior commanders were both uneasy about the interruption of the ever-important reserve training cycles and unable to comprehend how a solution could be found in the territories through purely military means.[107] In August 1988 Chief of

Staff Dan Shomron reportedly told the Knesset Foreign Affairs and Defense Committee that the IDF "cannot change Palestinian consciousness."[108]

The *intifada* also made inroads into the IDF's still-tight local-currency budgets. In July 1988 Defense Minister Yitzhak Rabin reportedly said that the direct costs of the *intifada* to the defense establishment had totaled 270 million shekels — a rate of 38.6 million shekels (about $25 million) a month.[109]

By 1988 the issue of the broad social costs involved in Israel's high levels of defense expenditure had started to be addressed in an interesting, though still muted, national debate. In December 1987 researcher Ariel Halperin argued that investment in the military industrial sector had actually caused a downturn in industrial growth rates. He therefore urged the government to reduce the size of the military industries.[110] In January 1988 Haifa University rector Gabriel Ben-Dor used an index called the Military Capital Inventory (MCI) to show that by 1984 the balance of military assets between Israel and all three of its Arab neighbors was "not a bad ratio." He argued that Israel should exploit the situation to keep its enemies at bay, "not with even more arms we can't afford but by statecraft. . . . This is the time to cut defense spending and concentrate on economic growth, techno-scientific progress, education and welfare," the rector urged.[111]

If the Israelis were faced with new and complex security challenges at the end of the 1980s, they could take some comfort from an impressive demonstration of their own techno-military wizardry in September 1988, when the Israeli Space Agency announced the country's first launch of an experimental satellite atop a three-stage, Israeli-made rocket booster. The initial reaction was to boast about this achievement, but within days there were signs of some debate over Israel's burgeoning space program, which also included development of another type of Israeli satellite — the Amos. By early October there were reports that some senior IDF commanders considered the Amos project another expensive white elephant like the Lavi.[112] A left-of-center daily noted in an editorial that "paradoxically enough, the launch of a satellite whose final price tag is estimated at $1 billion and an 8-million-shekel cut in the budget for higher education came at one and the same time" and urged that "great care should be taken not to have the satellite's launch revive the arms race in the Middle East."[113]

At the operational level, the space program promised to strengthen Israel's reconnaissance and real-time C^3I capabilities in battlefields both near and far from its own borders. By the end of 1988 Israeli military analysts were talking increasingly about the need to strengthen the long-range operational capabilities that had earlier been demonstrated in bombing raids in Iraq in 1981, in Tunis in 1985, and in the April 1988 assassination in Tunis of the PLO second-in-command, Khalil al-Wazir. Other elements of Israeli planning for a future long-range engagement included the continuing development of its Jericho missile program and the Arrow antitactical ballistic missile (ATBM) research and development program on which it was engaged in collaboration with the U.S. Strategic Defense Initiative (SDI). Building up Israel's long-range capabilities could help prepare the country for a contingency in which Iraqi, Saudi, or other capabilities might be committed to an anti-Israel war coalition. It would also increase Israel's ability to deter a Syrian attack.

Evolution of the Israeli-Syrian Deterrence Relationship, 1978–1989

In some respects, as has been noted, the strategic relationship between Israel and Syria mirrored at the local level the broader relationship of mutual nonconventional deterrence existing between the two superpowers. This fact was not widely recognized until the late 1980s, however, when some of the rhetoric of a primitive form of deterrence started appearing in utterances of leaders of Israel's military establishment. Thus, in July 1988 Defense Minister Rabin made the following statement:

> One of our fears is that the Arab world and its leaders might be deluded to believe that the lack of international reaction to the use of missiles and gases gives them some kind of legitimization to use them. They know they should not be deluded to believe that, because . . . if they are, God forbid, they should know we will hit them back 100 times harder.[114]

That statement had been made with regard to Iraq's recent use (against Iran) of missiles and chemical weapons, but the message for a Syria constantly accused by Israeli leaders of building a hostile chemical weapons and missile force could hardly have been clearer. By September 1988 Rabin was expressing his confidence that "our capacity to hit the Syrian rear, and Syrian launch-sites, is many times greater than the Syrians' capacity to hit our rear." He judged that "Israel today has a good deterrent capability vis-à-vis the Syrian military threat."[115]

In the July discussion Rabin had concluded that "wars at present and in the future would be painful and costly. Even those wars we win would exact a painful price."[116] Chief of Staff Dan Shomron then admitted in September 1988 that "regardless of whether we initiate the war or not, the threat to the civilian population will exist in one form or another."[117] Thus, at least these two top national security decision makers gave the clear impression that they understood their deterrence relationship with Syria to be marked by some degree of mutuality, however asymmetrical. None of Israel's top leaders, however, seemed willing to say as much in public about Israel's vulnerability to Syrian capabilities as their military professionals were apparently willing to say to two trusted strategic analysts. These were Hirsh Goodman and W. Seth Carus, who in early 1990 wrote:

The paradox that confronts Israeli military planners
is that while they recognize that Israel will retain an
absolute military advantage over Syria and any likely
constellation of confrontation states, many believe
that Israel cannot in the final analysis win a war. . . .
No matter how victorious its forces may be in the
field, the costs are likely to far outweigh any gain. . . .
The cornerstone of Israel's strategic philosophy,
therefore, must be deterrence, and the main task of the
IDF will not be to win a war, but to prevent one from
happening.[118]

This language was strongly reminiscent of Bernard
Brodie's famous post–World War II prophecy concerning
the mission of the American military in a nuclear age. In
two important respects, however, the "deterrence equation"
that existed between Israel and Syria differed from that
which so long defined relations between the United States
and the Soviet Union. First, in the Israel-Syria theater,
unlike in the relationship between the superpowers, a major
border dispute remained unresolved. As Ze'ev Schiff
warned in a 1986 series of articles, "Damascus will not be
willing to accept the status quo forever, both in the Golan
and in Lebanon. Neither is it willing to accept separate
political accords concluded by other Arab countries with
Israel, leaving Syria on the outside, as was the case with
the Camp David agreements."[119] In December 1985, Defense Minister Rabin had warned: "I cannot be certain that
my logic and Syrian logic are one and the same"; in a 1988
interview he returned to the same theme, warning that Israel could not be sure that the logic of deterrence would
apply in Syria's case.[120]

Gauging Syrian intentions thus continued to be a close
concern for the Israelis in the late 1980s, even after some
of the other elements of a mutually deterrent relationship
were falling into place. This has never been an easy task.
Although President Asad's public pronouncements on strategic affairs have generally been marked by caution or clev-
erly crafted ambiguity, those of some of his close associates

have been more bellicose. In August 1989, for instance, Defense Minister Tlas told an Arab journalist:

> We are prepared for the expected Israeli attack, for which they will pay many times what they have bargained for. The war with Israel is welcome, as such a development is bound to make the Soviets take a more hardline stand toward Israel and bring them still closer to us. . . . Besides, a war with Israel will embarrass a good many pro-U.S. Arabs before their peoples and armies. For these reasons we do want war with Israel, as it would do us good. . . .

The journalist then asked an obvious question: "If you stand to gain and Israel and the United States to lose from this war, what is holding you back from starting it?" Tlas's reply to this reflected more of his president's customary caution:

> This is up to us to decide. Our preparedness and armaments and local, Arab, and international circumstances come into play. . . . It will be for us to set the timing and field of the war. We will not have any party drag us into a war, the place and timing of which are not decided by us.[121]

This quotation clearly indicates that the war-averse policy Syria pursued with respect to Israel throughout the decade was a result of effective Israeli deterrence, rather than merely Syrian goodwill.

A second important way in which the Israeli-Syrian deterrence relationship differed from that pertaining between the superpowers stemmed from the fact that in an all-out confrontation between the superpowers, the scale of assured destruction would be so massive as to render meaningless any measurement of marginal differences between the situations in each homeland. In the event of a confrontation between Israel and Syria, by contrast, Israel's possession of a nuclear arsenal gave it sufficient superiority over Syria that the degree of destruction assured in an all-out encounter between the two would remain significantly asymmetrical; Syria's national infrastructure was assured of "more" destruction than Israel's, though both would probably suffer extremely heavy losses. The only circumstances that could change this inequality would be Syria's acquisition of either its own matching nuclear capability, or an unconditional guarantee of an "extended deterrent" nuclear umbrella from outside, or Israel's renunciation of its nuclear capabilities. During the period under study, Syria acquired none of these compensatory factors.[122] Therefore, Israel's superior capabilities at the nonconventional, heartland-busting level remained unchallenged, although questions raised about the relevance of its nuclear capabilities to any foreseeable battlefield encounter remained unanswered.[123]

Although the broad strategic asymmetry remained continuously in Israel's favor during the decade under study, there was a certain amount of dynamism in the degree of this asymmetry. This dynamism arose as much from the intangibles involved in any deterrence relationship—including each side's assessments of its opponent's interests and resolve, as well as from these local parties' assessments of superpower behavior—as it did from any new hardware acquisitions the parties made in the nonconventional field.

In the absence of any total confrontation between Israel and Syria in the period studied, the two sides had to gauge these intangibles from their recollections of the record of the earlier wars of 1967 and 1973, as well as from the more limited encounters that continued to occur. From 1978 through 1981, the military situation in all three of the conventional arenas in which the two sides interacted remained stable. Then, in 1981 the Red Lines agreements in Lebanon witnessed the small erosion that was precipitated by the missile crisis; that erosion was followed by the massive assault launched against the agreements by Israeli Defense Minister Sharon the following year. From 1981 through 1985, the confrontation between Israel and Syria was played out very visibly, and with great fluidity and destruction, within the Lebanese arena.

By implementing his 1982 Big Plan in Lebanon, Sharon managed—however briefly—to shift the political-military balance within that subtheater decisively in Israel's favor. Despite his achievement, however, he seriously overreached two important components of his country's overall strategic capability—its domestic consensus and its relationship with outside supporters, primarily the U.S. government. His action also forced the Syrians to take two decisive courses of action. One of these, the counterattack in Lebanon, succeeded within two years in reversing the momentary political gains Sharon had registered there. The other was Syria's pursuit of the greatest arms buildup the country had ever witnessed.

By 1985 these developments in Lebanon, in Syria, and inside Israeli society had had the effect of reducing, but not eradicating, the degree of strategic asymmetry between Israel and Syria. The period 1985 through 1989 witnessed further marginal shifts in the strategic equation—initially in Israel's favor as the IDF returned its operations to an even keel, and as Syria started hitting resource constraints in its arms buildup; then, from late 1987, slightly away from Israel as the new factor of the *intifada* intervened; and then back toward Israel as Syria became bogged down in Lebanon. Throughout all of these marginal shifts, however, Israel still clearly retained the strategic upper hand with respect to Syria.

During the short period in late 1985 and early 1986, when it may well have seemed to the Syrian rulers that they were making real progress toward attaining strategic parity, two incidents occurred that may (but need not) be interpreted as Syrian probes of the strategic environment. The first of these incidents occurred in November 1985, when the Syrians once again deployed SAM-6 batteries inside eastern Lebanon. As in 1981, this move provoked strong Israeli protest. But (as was also true in 1981) the

Israelis had themselves precipitated the Syrian move – on this occasion by shooting down two Syrian MiGs inside Syrian airspace. This time around, the crisis was fairly rapidly resolved. Both sides made concessions: the Syrians removed their SAMs from inside Lebanon (though they kept some they had placed inside Syria near their border with Lebanon), and the Israelis changed their flight paths over the Bekaa to avoid further mishaps.[124] The outcome was thus a return to the terms of the pre-1981 Red Lines agreement concerning who was allowed to do what in and over the Bekaa. Meanwhile, Asad had clearly signaled that he would resist any Israeli challenge along his own border with Lebanon.

The second possible Syrian probe occurred in April 1986, when a man called Nizar Hindawi, apparently a Syrian agent, was discovered to have tried to smuggle explosives aboard an Israeli flight leaving London. Fortunately, the explosives were discovered and removed before the flight took off. Hindawi then sought and received help from the Syrian embassy in London before turning himself in to the British police.[125] Most commentary about this affair has concluded that if the plane had blown up in midair, the fact that Hindawi's trail so clearly led to the Syrians would have constituted a clear casus belli for Israel.

Did the Hindawi affair indicate a new willingness on Asad's behalf to entertain the risks of going to war with Israel? The evidence is mixed. The Syrian president steadfastly disavowed Syrian involvement and argued that the entire plot had been concocted by the Israelis in an attempt to implicate Syria in a serious charge of international terrorism. For their part, the British investigators revealed that, although Asad himself was not directly implicated in planning Hindawi's operations, his chief of air force intelligence, Muhammed Khuly, clearly was. After the terrorist was convicted, the British broke relations with Syria over the affair and urged other Western nations to follow suit. Asad refused, however, to distance himself decisively from Khuly. Thus, although Asad himself was still not revealed to be someone who would engage in such clearly risky activity as planning the Hindawi operation, he did seem prepared to accept such activity from close associates.[126]

If the incidents of November 1985 and April 1986 are interpreted as Syrian probes of the strategic environment, then the lessons the Syrian planners learned from them must have been sobering, for in their wake Syrian behavior returned to its previous mode of cautious disinclination to engage militarily with the IDF; toward the end of 1986, as has been noted, resource constraints forced Syria to start mothballing some of its newly swollen order of battle. This allowed Israel once again to start increasing its strategic lead over Syria.

At the end of the 1980s, the governments in Israel and Syria continued to consider each other the source of the greatest military threat and to devote a high proportion of their national resources to ensuring that this threat would be adequately met. By the beginning of the 1990s, the new factor of Iraq's apparent reorientation toward the Arab-Israeli conflict also intervened, considerably complicating the strategic calculus for both Israel and Syria.

Despite the new uncertainties introduced by the Iraqi factor, several of the trends that marked the Israel-Syria balance in the 1980s appeared to be potentially useful in defining the prospects for the 1990s inside that balance, as well as – to a degree, at least – in the emerging strategic confrontation between Israel and Iraq. The most important of these trends was the uneasy coexistence between political immobility and mutual military deterrence that was evident in the Israeli-Syrian conflict in the 1980s. This situation offered no promise of long-term strategic stability. If, however, the outstanding issues of disagreement between the two parties could be seriously negotiated in good faith, then mutual military deterrence eventually might provide (as it had for the superpowers before them) a transition from a situation in which major wars were conceivable to one of genuine and stable coexistence.

During the 1980s in both Israel and Syria, national

governments were seen reining in previous arms buildups and standing down active forces even in the absence of major wars, progress toward peace, or other decisive political events. Both sides eventually began to realize that any future war between them would be immensely costly – for the "winner" as well as for the loser. On neither side, however, had this realization led to any clearly identifiable decision, by the end of the decade, to shift decisively away from this approach toward a more political solution to the issues outstanding between them. In summer 1987, the Syrian foreign minister was stressing, "We have no illusions about the possibility of peace in the region – the Israelis are not ready for it."[127] Meanwhile, Israeli Chief of Staff Shomron was pressed hard by a group of Israeli interviewers in September 1988 about whether he would be prepared to discuss "issues such as a partial withdrawal from the Golan Heights." His reply: "I do not want to go into that. The consensus is that we do not discuss this matter."[128]

How long beyond the end of the decade Israel's strategic decision makers could maintain this consensus remained open to question – particularly because of other emerging international political pressures that might push Israel and Syria toward a negotiation despite any respective reservations. One of these pressures was the thawing in global politics that accelerated so remarkably at the end of the 1980s. With the 45-year-old confrontation in Europe collapsing almost overnight into East-West cooperation, a continued state of hostility between Israel and Syria began to appear far less inevitable. Israel and Syria could also be pushed toward negotiation by the Israeli-Palestinian peace process that began hesitantly in 1988–1989. Another impetus to reopening the long-frozen real negotiations between Israel and all the Arab states, including Syria, might be provided precisely by the uncertainties newly introduced in 1990 by Iraq.

The failure of the two local actors, in the years from 1978 through 1989, to shift from a military to a political interaction can be attributed in part to the behavior of the superpowers over the preceding years. In the period under study, it is possible to identify the following decisions in which the role of the superpowers was crucial:

- Israel's decision, after the conclusion of the Camp David accords and the peace treaty with Egypt, not to stand down any proportion of its forces.
- Israel's decision to pursue the Big Plan and engage the Syrians in Lebanon.
- Israel's decision not to continue its pursuit of the Big Plan right up to the borders of Syria.
- Syria's decision to build up its forces considerably in the post-1982 years, but also its failure to attain the strategic parity with Israel that it sought.

In most of these cases, the crucial means of superpower intervention were arms supplies, although in the decision making over the 1982 fighting the granting or withholding of political support became the most important instrument. To understand the reason that the two superpowers acted as they did with regard to the Israel-Syria confrontation, as well as the prospects for reducing the tensions there in the 1990s, it is necessary first to discuss in depth the nature of the commitment each superpower had developed over the years to its local partner.

3

The U.S.-Israeli Relationship

**The Shift from the Moral to
the Strategic Relationship**

Israel's ability to exert influence within the American political system has been one factor distinguishing the U.S. relationship with Israel from that with any other participant in "regional conflicts." During the period under study, but especially during the eight years of the Reagan administration, the nature of the relationship changed significantly. These changes were apparent in both concrete policy decisions and the content of official U.S. rhetoric concerning Israel. The relationship changed from a U.S. moral commitment to Israel to one in which Israel was viewed as a strategic asset for the United States. This shift had important consequences for mutual attitudes toward the relationship, as well as for the parties' respective abilities to influence each other.

Initial traces of this shift in the nature of the relationship can be identified as early as the aftermath of the June 1967 Arab-Israeli war. Steven Spiegel, a political scientist at the University of California in Los Angeles, has noted of American attitudes in that earlier period that conservatives and military officials became more sympathetic to the Israelis. . . . The Israelis were now positively contributing to U.S. security: their combat experience and capture of Russian equipment provided information important to the American military in Vietnam. . . . Israel's new conservative sympathizers were more likely [than its previous more liberal supporters] to agree with its military approach to conducting foreign policy and with the need for advanced weaponry.[1]

It was against this background that President Lyndon B. Johnson secretly approved an increased exchange of intelligence with the Israelis. In early 1968 the Israelis increased their requests for U.S. military technology. Arguing their case for Johnson's approval of the sale of Phantom (F-4) fighter-planes was Yitzhak Rabin, their new ambassador to Washington and former chief of staff. His appointment can be seen as symbolic of the change in the tenor of the bilateral link.[2] In October Johnson decided to approve the Phantom sale. Amidst the pro-Israeli rhetoric generated by the U.S. presidential election of that year, he affirmed that he would not ask for any of the quid pro quos such as Israel's commitment to the principle of withdrawal from the occupied territories in return for peace, nor its agreement to sign the Nuclear Non-Proliferation Treaty (NPT) – both of which were being urged on him by his secretaries of state and defense.[3]

Under President Richard M. Nixon, the two governments became increasingly receptive to each other's strategic arguments.[4] In this atmosphere of growing mutual strategic admiration, U.S. military aid to Israel increased significantly. This was evident, first, in the U.S. budget for fiscal year 1971, when military aid (loans plus grants) increased from less than $100 million per year to an annual level higher than $300 million. Three years later, the level of military aid leapt again in the aftermath of the 1973 Middle East war. In the three fiscal years 1974 through 1976, military aid ran at a mean annual level exceeding $1.4 billion.[5]

Under President Gerald Ford, the level of U.S. military aid to Israel was brought back to $1.0 billion a year from FY 1977 on. But more power in foreign policy decision making was meanwhile devolving onto Secretary of State Henry Kissinger, who had already shown himself eager to maximize strategic aspects of the relationship with Israel. During Kissinger's vicarship of U.S. foreign policy, the United States and Israel first began to attend regular (though still subministerial) meetings on strategic issues. According to the director of the Pentagon's Office of Net Assessments, Andrew Marshall, it was in the mid-1970s that the Israelis requested the opening of high-level channels between the Pentagon and their Ministry of Defense to discuss strategic planning. Periodic meetings between the two sides started in 1976, while the Labor-led coalition was in office in Israel and Ford was president of the United States.[6]

President Jimmy Carter came into office in January 1977 with a position that was very supportive of Israel. In a departure from the views of his predecessors, however, Carter's attitude stemmed more from the traditional moral justifications for supporting Israel than from full-scale endorsement of Israel's strategic claims.[7] Under Carter, military aid to Israel was kept at the $1.0 billion mark — except for the single year 1979 when, in conjunction with the conclusion of the Camp David accords, the administration requested and received from Congress an additional $3.0 billion, which was earmarked for the costs associated with Israel's withdrawal from Sinai.[8] (Although Congress appropriated this sum in the FY 1979 budget, it appears that much of it was not consumed by Israel until 1981 or so — see chapter 2.) With this exception, Ford and Carter stabilized the military aid flow at a level somewhat lower than that of the immediate post-1973 years. The new level was, however, much higher in both current and constant dollars than that which prevailed before 1973. Thus, the level of U.S. military aid, as well as that of Israel's overall military budget, did not respond to the removal of Egypt from the

Arab-Israeli conflict by showing any significant reduction.

The contrast between Carter's view of Israel and that of his successor was stark. In an article published in August 1979, Ronald Reagan wrote of "Israel's geopolitical importance as a . . . military offset to the Soviet Union" and of its value as "perhaps the only remaining strategic asset in the region on which the United States can truly rely." The future president concluded that "only by full appreciation of the critical role the State of Israel plays in our strategic calculus can we build the foundation for thwarting Moscow's designs on territories and resources vital to our security and our national wellbeing."[9]

President Reagan's policies after coming into office were in line with this rhetoric. The wording of the article quoted here, moreover, reflected a theme that was strongly evident throughout the first years of his administration: namely, the president's tendency to view the Middle East (like all other regional issues) primarily through the prism of the East-West conflict. To this theme was added an emphasis on the threat posed by "international terrorism," which was magnified after the president himself was injured in an assassination attempt in Washington, D.C., only ten weeks after he assumed office. The perceived strength of the terrorist threat served to increase the value of strategic cooperation with an Israel that had won world renown for its counterterrorist effort.

Reagan's predilection for viewing Israel as a strategic asset was reinforced by many of his initial appointees to top positions. His vice president was George Bush, who had stated during the campaign that "it is in the strategic interest of the United States to maintain Israel's strength and security."[10] His first national security adviser, Richard V. Allen, had previously warmly endorsed the writings of the hawkish and pro-Israeli defense analyst Joseph Churba. To represent the United States at the United Nations, Reagan chose Jeane J. Kirkpatrick, who in 1982 described herself as "a very good friend of Israel." She also reassured her American Jewish audience that "there are a good many of us throughout the administration, beginning at the top."[11] Reagan's first secretary of state, Alexander M. Haig, was later to be described by the *Jerusalem Post*'s Wolf Blitzer as "a pro-Israel advocate in the administration."[12] (Haig viewed as his first goal in the Middle East the creation of a U.S.-Israeli-Arab "strategic consensus" that would confront the Soviet Union there; one of the earliest trips he made as secretary was an April 1981 visit to the Middle East in pursuit of this aim, in which he deliberately avoided visiting Syria. When it was clear that the Arabs would not enter into such an arrangement alongside Israel, he became the architect of the bilateral U.S.-Israeli Memorandum of Understanding or MOU on strategic cooperation that was concluded in November 1981.)

The major cabinet-level dissenter from the pro-Israeli chorus was, by all accounts, Secretary of Defense Caspar W. Weinberger. It was not that he was soft on the core issue of "the Soviet threat." Quite the opposite was true. But his view, which was reinforced by much of the institutional wisdom within both his own department and the State Department, was reportedly that countries such as Turkey, Egypt, and Saudi Arabia could make a greater contribution to sustaining the U.S. defense posture in the Middle East than could Israel.[13]

The Reagan administration's path toward establishing strategic links with Israel was not all smooth. Even before the conclusion of the 1981 MOU, the administration had several indications that its dealings with Israel might not be easy. In June 1981, in apparent contravention of U.S. legislation governing arms transfers abroad, Israeli planes supplied by the United States bombed the Iraqi nuclear facility in Baghdad. The following month, the Israeli Air Force (IAF) used other U.S.-supplied planes in its bombing of Palestinian targets in Beirut. And, in September 1981, Israeli Premier Menachem Begin outraged Reagan and embarrassed Haig when, during a state visit to Washington, he campaigned publicly in Congress and the press against the administration's plan to sell AWACS (airborne warning and control system) early-warning aircraft to Saudi Arabia.[14]

The administration continued to fight for congressional support of the AWACS sale; in October it won by a Senate vote of 52 to 48. The Israelis were quick to salvage what they could from their defeat—partially as a "compensation award" to them for having lost the AWACS battle, the administration in November responded to urgings from Israeli Defense Minister Ariel Sharon to conclude the MOU.[15]

Since the administration's earliest weeks in office, Haig and some of his staff in the State Department had reportedly been considering formalizing the strategic discussions with Israel that had continued since 1976. One former official close to this endeavor recalled that, although it was the Israeli side that provided the original push for formalization, "NSC and State came to feel that the American side should agree to this, because formalization would help to get the Pentagon on board."[16] Samuel Lewis, who as U.S. ambassador to Israel participated in many of these discussions, indirectly confirmed this assessment of the bureaucratic politics involved when he said that "Caspar Weinberger, who is nothing if not loyal to President Reagan, swallowed hard and took on the task of negotiating the details of this agreement."[17] (General Menachem Meron, Israel's military attaché in Washington at that time, would later recall that, in 1981, "America's professional military men were opposed to the MOU."[18])

In September 1981 State Department Counselor Robert C. McFarlane traveled to Israel and Egypt as Haig's envoy to conduct talks on strategic issues in both countries. In October Egypt's President Sadat was killed. Many of the American officials believed that this development only magnified the urgency of reaching a strategic agreement with Israel. The MOU was concluded at a meeting between Sharon and Weinberger in Washington at the end of November.

Under the MOU, planned strategic cooperation would

ward off "the threat to peace and security of the region caused by the Soviet Union or Soviet-controlled forces from outside the region introduced into the region."[19] The specificity with which the text spelled out that it was aimed against Soviet threats had been insisted on by the U.S. side, which was trying to allay the fears of those friends in the Arab world who feared that the strategic cooperation might be aimed against them. On the Israeli side, however, many strategic planners continued to worry about the implications for their country of identifying it with such an openly anti-Soviet effort. General Meron has noted that the Israeli negotiators succeeded in reducing the number of references to the Soviet threat from the dozen that had been in the original U.S. draft to a final total of seven, "but seven times it was mentioned just to make sure that all the Arab countries would not regard it as being an agreement against them."[20]

In concrete terms, the MOU provided for joint military exercises, including naval and air exercises in the eastern Mediterranean, cooperation in establishing and maintaining joint readiness activities, and establishing a joint supervisory council whose meetings would be chaired when possible by the secretary of defense and the minister of defense. In an interview broadcast by Jerusalem radio the next morning, however, Sharon opined that "Israel got most of what it wanted through this agreement."[21]

Some American supporters of the 1981 MOU had hoped that its conclusion might help to restrain Israel from rash actions that could destabilize American interests in the Middle East. They were soon to be proven wrong. On December 14, Premier Begin tabled the resolution in the Israeli Knesset extending Israeli law to the occupied Golan Heights. Four days after the resolution was passed, the State Department announced the suspension — but not cancellation — of the MOU. Begin's counterresponse was tough. Calling in U.S. Ambassador Samuel Lewis, he read him a vituperative lecture asking, "What kind of talk is this, 'punishing Israel'? Are we a vassal state of yours? Are we a banana republic?"[22]

Thus ended the first, abortive phase of formal strategic cooperation. Once the dust had settled from the Golan affair, however, relations were soon workable. The Americans were particularly grateful that the Israelis in April 1982 completed the final stage of withdrawal from Sinai that was a cornerstone of the Camp David process. Then, in May 1982 Sharon visited the United States where, according to Ze'ev Schiff and Ehud Ya'ari, he gave undeniable hints to Haig that the expected Israeli action in Lebanon might go beyond merely striking at the PLO.[23] Begin was scheduled to follow him in June.

In early June Begin and Sharon presented the United States with another surprise in the form of their massive invasion of Lebanon. Schiff wrote that, at last-minute Israeli cabinet meetings held before the invasion was launched, "it was clear to many Israeli ministers that based on what Washington was saying behind the scenes – unlike what it was saying in public – Israel was already assured of U.S. support."[24] Haig, whose position within the administration had been seriously eroding since early spring, hotly denied that any green light had been given to Israel. His own record, however, of the position he took in the spring 1982 meetings with the Israelis could very well have been interpreted that way by the Israeli side.[25] Israeli analyst Zvi Lanir later commented that the Reagan administration "did not realize its own responsibility in the affair. Israel went to war only after its leaders felt they had received American permission to do so." He explained that ever since the war of 1973 had brought home to Israelis the extent of their dependence on the United States, Israeli leaders would not make a war decision without getting an advance "blessing" from the Americans.[26]

As the IDF became bogged down around Beirut in late June, the Reagan administration was rent by a visceral split over the issue. This pitted Haig against national security adviser William P. Clark (who had replaced Richard Allen in January 1982), as well as against influential White House insiders such as Vice President George Bush and Chief of Staff James A. Baker III. Clark, who favored a tougher American attitude toward the Israeli action, prevailed over Haig in the last week of June, and on June 25 Reagan announced Haig's resignation.[27]

Haig was replaced as secretary of state by George P. Shultz, who had been labor secretary under Nixon and since then a top executive with Bechtel Inc. The circumstances of his arrival at the State Department, and his reputed business experience in the Arab world, provided some indication that Shultz might be less enamored of the Israelis than his predecessor. Certainly his first few weeks in office seemed to bear out that promise. The Israelis were forced to allow the PLO forces to make a relatively dignified exit from Beirut carrying sidearms. The U.S. government produced the first peace plan for the Arab-Israeli conflict ever issued explicitly in the president's name; the plan ruled out Israel's claims to sovereignty in the West Bank and Gaza. (The 1982 Reagan plan made no explicit mention of Syria's continuing grievance against the Israelis concerning the continuing occupation of the Golan Heights.) Then, following the revelation of September's refugee camp massacres in Beirut, the United States peremptorily ordered the Israelis to withdraw from the city, interposing the MNF-2 between the IDF and the city.

Over the year that followed September 1982, however, Shultz's actions seemed to indicate that he was beginning to share Haig's pro-Israeli point of view. Indeed, one of the interesting questions concerning U.S. policy toward Israel in the Reagan era focuses on why this came about. Some pro-Israeli analysts liked to describe what happened as the "return to realism" of a policy that had, at the time of the Reagan plan's announcement, been fundamentally unrealistic.[28] One such analyst, Martin Indyk, produced a list of additional factors that had led to Shultz's turnaround that probably correctly included the American consideration that, "at the end of 1982, Congress made clear that it would not support a campaign of diplomatic pressure [against Israel]." Indyk also mentioned the effect on Shultz of the replacement of Begin and Sharon by Yitzhak Shamir and

Moshe Arens as Israel's premier and defense minister, respectively.[29] An additional factor was the influence on the new secretary of a number of key pro-Israeli aides in the State Department. An especially crucial role in this respect was played, according to several administration insiders, by Under Secretary Lawrence S. Eagleburger.[30]

Whatever his motives, by April 1983 Shultz had decided to cut a deal with the Israelis over Lebanon, giving them the go-ahead to reach an agreement with Lebanese President Amin Gemayel for which the Americans would only subsequently seek support from the Syrians. This approach would confront Syria with a diplomatic fait accompli concerning the crucial issue of the future security regime in Lebanon. This decision by Shultz, and the U.S.-Israeli-Lebanese agreement that resulted from it on May 17, defused the confrontation that had been brewing between the United States and Israel in Lebanon. What it did not achieve was any stabilization of the situation in Lebanon, where the outraged Syrians stepped up their support for the agreement's many local opponents. And, in October 1983, a radical Lebanese Shi'ite grouplet orchestrated the devastating truck-bomb attack against the Marine barracks in Beirut.

Any effective response on the part of the Reagan administration to this challenge was constrained militarily by the reluctance of the Department of Defense (DoD) to commit any more forces to a mission in Lebanon that they already considered dangerously ill-defined. Politically, the U.S. reaction was more clear-cut. Merely six days after the explosion, President Reagan signed National Security Decision Directive 111 (NSDD-111), which reinstated the concept of strategic collaboration with Israel. Two days after the NSDD was signed in Washington, Eagleburger was sent to Israel to discuss it with the new Israeli premier, Yitzhak Shamir. Eagleburger reportedly told his host that "the president wanted to discuss strategic cooperation in Lebanon, in the Middle East generally, and everywhere." In what was described as "a kind of political down payment,"

Eagleburger reportedly informed the Israelis that part of the $1.7 billion they were now receiving annually in military aid could henceforth be spent on developing the Lavi, rather than—as is normally the case with Foreign Military Sales (FMS) appropriations—being limited to purchasing U.S. products.[31]

The October 1983 NSDD proved to be a much more durable basis for the development of U.S.-Israeli strategic cooperation than its precursor of 1981. When Premier Shamir visited Washington in November, the two sides agreed to establish a formal Joint Political-Military Group (JPMG) that would convene every six months. President Reagan announced that the JPMG would "give priority to our mutual interests posed by increased Soviet involvement in the Middle East. Among the specific areas to be considered are combined planning, joint exercises, and requirements for prepositioning of U.S. equipment in Israel."[32]

The JPMG held its first meeting in January 1984, and over the next four years its achievements in shepherding increased strategic cooperation between the two governments appeared impressive. Naval vessels from the U.S. Sixth Fleet started making regular port calls to Haifa; the United States leased 25 Kfir C-1 fighters from Israel to simulate Soviet MiG planes in combat training; fleets from the two countries held joint antisubmarine warfare (ASW) maneuvers and passing exercises in the eastern Mediterranean; Sixth Fleet aviators conducted bombing practice against targets in Israel's Negev desert. In May 1986 Israel became the third signatory, after Britain and West Germany, to the SDI research and development program; the FY 1987 DoD budget bill reportedly authorized approximately $70 million for prepositioning U.S. war matériel in Israel; and in July 1986, Israel agreed to the installation of Voice of America transmitters, which would beam U.S. programming into the southern parts of the Soviet Union.[33]

The total volume of FMS aid to Israel rose only slightly in the wake of the October 1983 decision, from $1.7

billion in the FY 1983 budget to a constant annual level of $1.8 billion in the latter half of the decade. The Israeli military establishment, however, extracted clear benefits from at least four other developments in the U.S. military aid program in the post-NSDD era. First, the proportion of FMS funds given in the form of a straight grant, rather than a guaranty loan, was raised from a pre-NSDD level of 40 to 50 percent to 100 percent. Then a clearly defined and larger share of the FMS funds could be spent on "offshore procurement"—that is, purchases from the Israeli defense industry (in the FY 1988 budget this amount was $400 million). In addition, another part of each FMS grant, totaling $150 million in each of the FY 1988 and FY 1989 budgets, was designated as "directed offsets," forcing U.S. contractors supplying Israel to spend that amount on purchases of spares and subsystems inside Israel. (Israel's total take of these last two categories of offshore FMS funds between FY 1976 and FY 1989 would come to $6.5 billion, much of it spent on the Merkava tank and the Lavi.) And finally, Israel received further funding under approximately 20 DoD line items other than the FMS budget. This was the case, for example, with the 54 percent share it won in FY 1987 of the Foreign Weapons Evaluation Program appropriation,[34] as well as with the funding of its ATBM system from the SDI budget, which would reportedly bring another $480 million of DoD funds into Israel over three years.[35]

In December 1987 the flow of U.S. aid to the Israeli military establishment was notched even higher when Yitzhak Rabin, now defense minister, signed a further MOU with the United States, formally designating Israel as a "major non-NATO ally." This category of states had been created by Congress the previous year. It was publicly listed as including Israel, Egypt, South Korea, Japan, and Australia; however, when the House of Representatives tried to list specific weapons systems to receive funding under this program, all six of them were Israeli. The terms of the December 1987 agreement reportedly included joint research and development programs and increased U.S. procurement of Israeli-manufactured military products.[36] By 1988 purchases of Israeli-manufactured defense matériel by the U.S. military totaled $300 million – increased from $9.4 million five years earlier.[37]

When Secretary Shultz addressed the annual convention of the American Israel Public Affairs Committee (AIPAC) in May 1987, he thus had some grounds for his boast that "America's support for Israel has never been stronger or more steadfast."[38] By FY 1989, according to one researcher, the dollar figure for U.S. government support of the Israeli military establishment had reached $2.3 billion – though the FMS component of this was still tied at $1.8 billion.[39]

The Israeli government's achievement in gaining access to U.S. resources under the rubric of "strategic cooperation" was especially impressive because it occurred during a period when U.S.-Israeli relations were rocked by numerous political developments that in the context of any country other than Israel would have proved extremely damaging in Washington. In November 1985 the Jewish-American spy Jonathan Pollard was arrested as he tried to seek shelter inside the Israeli embassy in Washington; the following year, he was convicted on charges of having passed vast quantities of secret U.S. documents to a spy ring sanctioned by the Israeli government, possibly compromising some of the most sensitive U.S. intelligence-gathering activities. At the end of 1986, the "Irangate" scandal in Washington revealed the strong participation of Israeli officials and arms dealers in Robert McFarlane and Oliver North's ill-fated "arms for hostages" deal. Less dramatic than these developments but of equally detrimental potential impact on the U.S.-Israeli relationship were such disagreements as those over the Arab-Israeli peace process, Israel's ties to South Africa, the massive cost overruns (at the U.S. taxpayer's expense) on the Lavi, and Israeli technician Mordechai Vanunu's October 1986 revelations concerning the status of Israel's nuclear weapons program.[40]

These far-reaching political and diplomatic disagreements seemed barely to dent the ongoing strategic relationship. Even the Pollard affair seemed to have little immediate impact. As General Meron recalled, "The next meeting of the JPMG was planned to be held in Washington one week after the blowout of the Pollard affair. I expected it to be postponed or cancelled. It was not. It was held as planned."[41]

In early 1988 one of the first achievements of the Palestinian *intifada* was to spur Secretary Shultz into yet another round of Arab-Israeli peacemaking. This diplomatic effort, like its predecessor six years earlier, failed to address the Syrian-Israeli conflict, keeping its focus on the more newsworthy Israeli-Palestinian issue. One of Shultz's early objectives in this effort was to extract a commitment from Israel, Jordan, and the Palestinians to accept the "land-for-peace" trade embodied in Security Council Resolution 242 as applicable on the West Bank and Gaza fronts. Israeli Premier Shamir refused to give such a commitment (as did, at that stage, the PLO). Some of Shamir's domestic critics warned that his intransigence might affect the flow of U.S. strategic goods to Israel, as had happened under earlier U.S. administrations; they were proved wrong. In April 1988 Israeli defense analyst Dore Gold wrote of the relationship between the military-strategic and political-diplomatic tracks in the Reagan administration's policy toward Israel, "As strategic ties with Israel came to be perceived as an American interest, it made no sense to condition their growth on diplomatic process [progress?] in the area of Arab-Israeli negotiations."[42] In May 1988 the United States signed yet another strategic MOU with Israel.

Shultz's efforts to restart the Arab-Israeli peace process came to naught in 1988. Before he left office, however, he was able to leave one major legacy to the diplomacy of the region. On December 14, 1988, he and President Reagan judged that PLO Chairman Yasir Arafat had finally met the conditions set by Henry Kissinger in 1975 for the United States to begin a dialogue with the PLO.

The first talks took place with the U.S. ambassador in Tunis almost immediately.

At that stage, the Israelis had just been through another round of inconclusive general elections. On December 22 the two largest parliamentary blocs, Labor and Likud, were able to reach a coalition agreement that explicitly stated, "Israel will not negotiate with the PLO," and notably made no mention of "land for peace."[43]

When George Bush came into office as forty-first president of the United States, the first indications were that his administration would follow the lead established by its predecessor in stressing the military and strategic aspects of the relationship with Israel. Throughout Bush's first year in office, however, the *intifada* continued to rage, and the Israeli government continued to stall on the "land for peace" issue. This raised with increasing acuteness the question of whether the Bush administration could continue to make no link between the ongoing strategic and aid relationships with Israel, on the one hand, and the continuing political disagreements between the two sides, on the other.[44]

In September 1989 in intriguing remarks that may have signaled a shift back toward the more "moral" prism through which pre-Reagan administrations had viewed Arab-Israeli issues, Assistant Secretary of State for Near Eastern and South Asian Affairs John Kelly told a conference of the Washington Institute for Near East Policy:

> In reviewing speeches of the Bush and Reagan administrations, I noticed that no senior American official had spoken much about the human dimension. . . . It is certainly the business of the U.S. government to look after U.S. interests in a clear-sighted and hardheaded way. But that does not mean that we must ignore humanitarian issues.[45]

Push Factors and Pull Factors

If the U.S. government was generally eager, under the two Reagan administrations, to strengthen the military aspects of its relationship with Israel, this feeling was also being strongly stimulated by the Israelis and some of their American friends.

In 1977, as noted in chapter 2, political power in Israel had passed from the Labor alignment to the right-wing Likud bloc. Whereas Labor had traditionally had many supporters among both Jews and non-Jews in the liberal Democratic camp in the United States, Likud's arrival in power in 1977 caused some American friends of Israel to fear that Israel was starting to lose its moral appeal. In late 1979, for example, the former president of the World Zionist Organization, Nahum Goldmann, publicly expressed his regret that "Israel is losing its moral qualification and is becoming only a small, aggressive state . . . thus losing the respect and the admiration of the larger part of world public opinion."[46]

In his 1985 book *Between Washington and Jerusalem, Jerusalem Post* correspondent Wolf Blitzer recalled that "it was not all that long ago when most Americans tended to cite primarily moral and emotional reasons for their support of Israel. . . . The strategic basis for the American-Israeli alliance was seldom cited." He then described one of the factors that changed this situation:

> The case for stressing the strategic side of the story has intensified in recent years. Israeli officials themselves have encouraged this trend, fearing that the massive sums of U.S. military and economic assistance to Israel might cease to be acceptable to the American public and Congress unless explained in such a hard-nosed way. If Israel were to be demonstrated to provide a useful military and strategic service to the United States on the other hand, the aid becomes justified on the basis of self-interest as well as national morality.[47]

The Israeli government's lead in deemphasizing Israel's moral appeal to U.S. public opinion was followed by pro-Israeli American personalities such as former AIPAC director Morris J. Amitay, who at a 1983 conference declared: "Moral authority has very little influence in politics.

Few would attempt to convince a congressman to vote for an aid bill for Israel with an appeal on behalf of Israel's 'moral authority.' Rather, I would make an appeal based on Israel's value."[48]

Israel's strategic arguments were enthusiastically perpetuated by Thomas Dine, who succeeded Amitay as AIPAC executive director in 1980. Dine's first big fight on AIPAC's behalf was the 1981 campaign against the Saudi AWACS deal. Although he lost that one, he immediately thereafter set about arming himself and his supporters with the kinds of arguments needed to ensure that never again would AIPAC lose a big fight over a Middle Eastern strategic issue. He hired a former RAND Corporation strategic analyst, Steven Rosen, as AIPAC's director of research and information, and set him and other strategic analysts to work producing a series of pamphlets advertising Israel's strategic values to each of the U.S. services.[49] In the first of these pamphlets, Rosen concluded that "Israel offers clear and substantial advantages as a prepositioning site for U.S. projection forces." A later pamphlet argued to its U.S. Navy readers that "Israel would . . . require no more than 1200 combat sorties to destroy the entire Soviet fleet in the region. . . . If Israel had no other concerns, this could be accomplished in a single day."[50]

These kinds of arguments received a ready hearing in some parts of the State Department and the DoD – a fact that was even more surprising because both of these agencies had historically been concerned about the broader strategic costs to the United States of tying its strategic posture too closely to that of Israel. What had changed in each of them with the advent of the Reagan presidency was the appointment to high-level positions of numerous individuals who seemed predisposed to sympathize with the arguments of Israel's strategic salesmen. These included Secretary of State Haig himself, who encouraged the legitimation of the "strategic Israel" argument, a phenomenon that has outlasted Haig's tenure in the State Department.

The presence in crucial State, Pentagon, and National Security Council (NSC) slots of individuals who were willing to sympathize with Israel's battery of strategic arguments provided essential agency-level backup to President Reagan, whose instincts were already deeply pro-Israeli. The effects of this combination in determining U.S. Middle East policy have correctly been described by writer Richard Straus as "revolutionary." Straus recalled that AIPAC's founder, I. L. Kenen, had described his organization's mission as being "to lobby the Congress to tell the president to overrule the State Department." Perceptively, Straus asked in 1986, "But what happens when the State Department doesn't need to be overruled?"[51]

The Strategic Arguments Assessed

Throughout the mid-1980s, numerous Israeli officials and pro-Israeli American scholars (though noticeably fewer Israeli strategic scholars) spoke and wrote extensively about the strategic benefits Israel could provide to the United States through enhanced collaboration. In 1987, for example, Ariel Sharon maintained that, whereas Soviet power was balanced in Europe by NATO and in Asia by the Chinese, "the only place where there is no organization dedicated to this end is the Middle East. The counter-Soviet balance here is provided by Israel."[52] In a 1986 presentation, Laborite Defense Minister Yitzhak Rabin gave a slightly different assessment. Although he did point out the strategic benefits that Israel could provide to the United States, he stressed that "the first layer" of the relationship still lay in the moral realm of shared values—that issues concerning the superpower rivalry constituted only a subsidiary "second layer."[53]

One of the most comprehensive cases made in the American scholarly community for Israel as a net provider of strategic benefits to the United States was presented in a fall 1986 article by Steven Spiegel. He wrote:

> Israel can be viewed in the global military context
> from five perspectives: its intelligence techniques, the
> implications of its battlefield experiences, the combina-
> tion of a tight defense budget and a penchant for inno-
> vation, the effect of its activities on the calculations of
> Soviet planners, and the impact of its military perfor-
> mance on the reputation of U.S. arms.[54]

Spiegel's verdict was that, in each of these five fields, a
close relationship with Israel offered clearcut benefits to
the United States. An additional argument, not made by
Spiegel but offered in a more apologetic spirit by other
Americans favoring close strategic ties with Israel, was
that such ties offered the United States more hope of being
able to restrain an Israeli military establishment that
might otherwise evade U.S. control.[55] These six arguments
for close strategic ties thus need to be examined.

Spiegel described Israeli intelligence as "widely regarded as the best in the Middle East." "Shared information," he said, "has enabled the United States to save on
training, deploying fewer intelligence operatives and utiliz-
ing fewer facilities."[56] It was apparently true that in one of
the cases to which he referred—acquisition of Nikita
Khrushchev's historic speech at the 20th Soviet Communist Party Congress—Israel's Mossad intelligence organization played a crucial role. Some of the other achievements he cited were less clearcut. Warnings of possible
assassination attempts against pro-Western Arab leaders
such as King Hussein or Anwar Sadat, for example, are
common in the Middle East and have come from other
quarters as well as Israel.

Reliance on Israel as America's eyes and ears in the
Middle East was never something most members of the
U.S. intelligence community were prepared to accept, despite the decades-long relationship between the Mossad
and the CIA's former chief of counterintelligence, James
Angleton.[57] Indications that reliance on Israeli institutions
might be harmful for the United States were never stronger

than during the Lebanon crisis of summer 1982, when Secretary Haig appeared to take at face value General Sharon's claims that he could rout the PLO and install a pro-Western government in Beirut without causing any disruption to Western interests in the region.[58]

U.S. officials involved in the strategic collaboration with Israel give Israel varying amounts of credit in the intelligence field. Director of the DoD Office of Net Assessments Andrew Marshall judged that it was valuable for the United States "to share the Israelis' understanding of the governments and societies of the region."[59] "Where is the line of their effectiveness?" asked another Defense Department official. "The closer in any area is to them, the better their intelligence is; and the further away, the spottier it is. But we have to remember that their assessments reflect their national goals, so Americans should always hold them up to a strong light." A third ranking Pentagon official, interviewed in 1989, placed the intelligence exchanges at the head of the list of benefits derived by the United States from the strategic collaboration, though he added, "The Israelis get more out of this than we do."[60]

The lessons learned from Israel's battlefield experience demonstrated, according to Spiegel, "the relative utility or weaknesses of established weapons" and revealed "the latest innovations of the Soviets."[61] This last claim is somewhat exaggerated because the Soviets have always been much more conservative about transferring their state-of-the-art military technology to friends in the Middle East than has the United States. The result of this imbalance was that during the 1982 Lebanon fighting, for example, the Israelis learned much about spooking the radars of Soviet-built SAM-6 missiles in the Bekaa Valley. The SAM-6 was a 15-year-old system, however, and in spooking it, the Israelis revealed much useful data to the Soviets concerning the capabilities of front-line NATO systems such as the E-2C Hawkeye, the F-16 fighter, and the Shrike and other precision-guided missiles used.[62] The diplomatically worded judgment of one high-level Pentagon official concerning the Israelis' compromise of NATO technology in this encounter was that "Israel has a very special situation. We might have preferred to protect that technology until we were in a more sensitive situation."[63]

Both the Soviets and the United States were able to learn lessons from the Bekaa air-defense battles that would help them in planning for the much broader-scale conventional front line in Central Europe. But the Soviets' lessons were probably more valuable and were acquired at smaller cost in terms of compromising their own systems than were those that the United States was able to learn. Meanwhile, as one DoD official monitoring the strategic relationship with Israel reported, the lessons Israel's battle experiences provide for U.S. force planners are "earned the hard way" in terms of other U.S. inducements. "We do get some useful lessons from Israeli experience," one non-Pentagon defense analyst familiar with the region observed, "but we have to extract them with difficulty. And the cost to us is tremendous."[64]

Israel's combination of a tight defense budget and a penchant for innovation, Spiegel wrote, "creates intriguing solutions to conventional defense problems at lower costs."[65] At some levels of technology this might well be true. At the high-technology end of the strategic spectrum, however, the creativity of the Israeli defense industry has occasionally seemed to be directed more to creative bookkeeping — the kind that in the context of U.S. defense contractors would undoubtedly have aroused the ire of the U.S. Congress — than to actual defense solutions.

The prime example of this was provided by the ill-fated Lavi project. The DoD official who supervised the final effort to bring standard U.S. cost-estimating procedures to bear on the project, Dov Zakheim, later argued that the entire affair, and the formal strategic cooperation that had allowed close U.S. scrutiny of the project, would ultimately prove beneficial to Israeli security because Israel's military R&D establishment thereby became subjected to far more rigorous cost-scrutiny procedures than any it had previously encountered.[66] Whatever the value of this argument, the Lavi affair, and its $1.3 billion cost to the U.S. taxpayer between 1980 and 1986, could scarcely be said to have been in the interests of the United States.[67] Spiegel's contention that "the United States inevitably benefits in its larger [defense] programs from sharing Israeli concepts and ideas" would thus seem open to serious challenge.[68]

Concerning the effect of Israel's activities on the calculations of Soviet planners, Spiegel could actually have made a better case than he did in this article because one focus of intense concern to Soviet planners is the question of Israel's nuclear capabilities.[69] But Spiegel remained silent about its nuclear capabilities, as did most of Israel's other U.S. supporters. The first argument he used was that concerning the lessons learned during the Bekaa Valley battles between Israel and Syria in 1982. His judgment concerning the air defense battle was that "about 20 percent of [the Soviets'] entire defense budget" had been nullified when their front-line air defense systems were compromised in the Bekaa.[70] This conclusion was based, however, on the premise that the Syrians had had front-line Warsaw Pact systems destroyed during the Bekaa fighting, which they did not. The conclusion, therefore, is scarcely convincing.

The second argument Spiegel adduced seemed more valid and has formed the basis for more visible U.S. coordination with the Israeli military than has the air defense issue. This argument concerned Israel's naval and air capabilities in the eastern Mediterranean. Interviews with current and former DoD, State Department, and NSC analysts reveal that for the United States the collaboration in the eastern Mediterranean has seemed to be the most beneficial element of the strategic cooperation with Israel. (In a 1988 paper, domestic policy expert Stuart Eizenstat listed eastern Mediterranean considerations above counter-Syrian considerations in building the case for enhanced strategic cooperation.)

The eastern Mediterranean, however, is not an area of

primary concern to U.S. strategic planners. As one defense
analyst on Capitol Hill described it, "The East Mediterranean is a sideshow to the Persian Gulf oilfields or the Suez
Canal.[71] One pro-Israeli analyst formerly with the NSC portrayed U.S.-Israeli collaboration in the eastern Mediterranean as important in providing air cover to U.S. sea lines
of communication (SLOCs) with the Gulf. A high-level Pentagon official dealing with these issues, however, judged
that the United States "cannot use the Eastern Mediterranean cooperation with Israel with respect to the Gulf
region."[72] This judgment seems realistic because not only
would direct military involvement with Israel be rejected
by all the Gulf states under now-foreseeable circumstances,
but it also remains extremely questionable whether, in the
event of any military confrontation of global proportions,
Israel would be ready to divert its military resources away
from its own immediate defense.

Thus, although the naval collaboration in the eastern
Mediterranean was the most visible of the U.S. joint strategic ventures with Israel, its contribution to worldwide U.S.
military planning was extremely limited. (For their parts,
defense analysts Hirsh Goodman and W. Seth Carus questioned the value to Israel of at least two of the centerpieces
of the collaboration in the eastern Mediterranean — the Saar
V missile-boat and new Israeli submarines.[73]) From the
U.S. point of view, meanwhile, the contribution Israel
might make in the eastern Mediterranean was still limited
by the fact that Israel had not entered into any formal
treaty obligation to commit its forces to the Western effort
in the event of a global war against the Soviet Union.[74]

The last of Spiegel's five claims, regarding the impact
of Israel's military performance on the reputation of U.S.
arms, is primarily of interest to those who seek to maximize
U.S. military sales worldwide. Many even in this group,
however, question Spiegel's implied claim that Israel's actions are of net benefit to the U.S. arms industry. According to nearly all the U.S. officials interviewed, the major
problem has been that, although Israel's battlefield performance may have enhanced the reputation of U.S. arms, the

actions of Israel's supporters in the U.S. Congress have nevertheless ensured that few Third World countries can afford to buy these arms, however great their reputation.

The problem here lies in Israel's tendency to consume most of the available FMS money, which is what the United States uses to lend to that majority of those customers who cannot (as the Saudis can) pay cash for their purchases. In FY 1986, for example, congressional earmarking of FMS funds for particular countries, including Israel, still left approximately $2 billion for the Pentagon to allocate at its discretion. Two years later, that figure had shriveled to between $200 and $300 million, according to one Pentagon analyst.[75] Pentagon analysts have estimated that the United States had to stop giving security assistance to "some 30 or 40 countries" to keep the level of military aid to Israel and Egypt at the level that became institutionalized subsequent to Camp David. Net Assessment's Andrew Marshall stated, "My first impression is that Israeli arms aid gobbles up a large fixed amount of money. The main thing one hears is about the constraints on foreign aid money, and the amount which is earmarked for Israel and Egypt."[76]

The last argument in favor of the formal strategic links between Israel and the United States that should be assessed is that such links increase the U.S. ability to control Israel's military actions. One of the most forthright proponents of this argument, a former NSC analyst, was frank in admitting that in the case of the 1981 MOU, "it never worked out that way, because of Lebanon." He explained: "We didn't realize what we were dealing with in Sharon." This analyst's more modest version of what the United States might hope to achieve with the post-1983 iteration of strategic collaboration was that "it might develop a stake in the relationship on behalf of *both* sides." He noted, however, that although this had been shown to be true "to some extent" in the case of the Labor Alignment and the IDF, it had not been demonstrated so much in the case of Likud.[77]

That this more modest aim might be the maximum

that the United States could expect from the relationship was indicated in a presentation given in July 1986 by Menachem Meron, who had seen service both in the Israeli embassy in Washington and as director-general of Israel's Ministry of Defense. Referring to the 1981 MOU, Meron said, "Washington believed that because of the MOU, there would be no more 'surprises' or unilateral moves on Israel's part. That was very far from the Israeli perception." Referring to the difference between the 1981 and 1983 versions of collaboration, he noted with apparent satisfaction that "there was the realization that local powers can, in some cases, possess inherent advantages over a superpower."[78]

Some systematic consideration should also be given, however briefly, to the actual and potential downside costs to the United States of the close strategic relationship with Israel. The relationship has, as noted above, resulted in some compromise of U.S. and NATO military technology and operations to the Soviets. One must also assume that, because no intelligence community anywhere can be considered leakproof, there is a chance that close intelligence coordination with Israel may have resulted in compromise of intelligence data and methods to the Soviets.

One high-level Pentagon official interviewed for the present study pointed out that risks of such compromise exist in any alliance relationship. He noted, however, that Israel differed from other U.S. allies both because of the special aggressivity of the Israeli defense industry in obtaining advanced U.S. technology and because of the existence of a strong political push factor, coming from organized public opinion and from the U.S. Congress, that has propelled successive administrations into close strategic ties with Israel. This official considered, however, that the principal downside cost to U.S. national security from the relationship with Israel stemmed not from the risk of compromise of U.S. secrets but from the extent to which the relationship curtailed U.S. links with the moderate Arab states. He added further significant nuance to this view when he noted that "dealing with Israel on issues of arms transfers to the Arabs is one matter; but the real difficulties come from dealing with a Congress which on this issue is more pro-Israeli than the Israelis themselves."[79]

Former Assistant Secretary for International Security Affairs Richard Armitage noted in a 1988 interview that one result of congressional and public pressure against arms sales to Arab countries has been that pro-Western Arab states became less stable because of the fear engendered by their inability to obtain their basic defense needs from the United States. In several cases, they have also turned elsewhere for the systems they wanted — a development that the United States also regards as less stable because the weapons of other countries come with fewer follow-on controls. "We end up losing political capital in the Middle East," he concluded. "We lose actual capital, and we lose influence. Because of these factors, and also because of the lack of control over some Arab weapons systems, the whole area is slightly less stable."[80]

The Israeli Debate

It is an irony of history that, in precisely the same period that Israel's "strategic salesmen" in the United States were having their biggest impact on official policy (from 1983 through 1987), the strategic studies community in Israel itself was wracked by the post-Lebanon debate. The community questioned many basic assumptions about the desirability for Israel of the ceaseless buildup of Israeli armed might that was being so effectively advocated by those very salesmen.

Some major aspects of the Israeli strategic debate, inasmuch as it concerned the country's domestic priorities, have been described in chapter 2. Another part of the debate there, however, focused on the nature of the U.S.-Israeli relationship, and especially the effect the relationship was having on the strategic planning of both sides. Feisty as ever, Ariel Sharon asserted in 1987 that "both sides have no alternative. The United States has no ally like Israel, and vice versa."[81]

Sharon's point of view was rebutted by Israeli political scientist Gabriel Sheffer, who wrote:

> From a purely strategic viewpoint, Israel's capability to assist the United States seems limited to certain parts of the Middle East, the best indication of this being its non-existent or marginal role in the Iran-Iraqi war, in the continuing Egyptian-Sudanese contro- versy, and in various attempts to check Libyan adven- tures abroad.[82]

For his part, Jaffee Center Director Aharon Yariv regret- ted in an interview that many in Sharon's Likud bloc seemed convinced that Israel was bringing substantial strategic benefits to the United States, and that some of Israel's supporters inside the United States were reinforc- ing them in this claim, which he considered exaggerated.[83]

Ze'ev Schiff also pointed to the excessive confidence of some Israelis on this score:

> The deepening of the [U.S.-Israeli] strategic ties, to- gether with the growth in aid, has created, perhaps inevitably, a sense of over-confidence in many Israelis, the belief that what exists between the two countries today can be taken for granted. . . . Even if Israel were to shun friendly advice from Washington and ignore U.S. interests, according to this belief, there would be no American reaction. . . . There are some extremist groups in Israel who believe that the U.S. cannot af- ford to desert Israel, regardless of what the latter does.[84]

In a 1988 interview, the Jaffee Center's Shai Feldman meanwhile judged that the strategic links with the United States had brought great benefits to Israel, both materially and in terms of enhancing Israel's capacity to deter its foes. "But there have been costs," he added. "There has been the

perception of Israel elsewhere in the world as being allied
to an imperial power; and the overwhelming benefits of the
alliance have enabled Israel to avoid difficult choices."[85]
Israeli economics writer Shlomo Ma'oz noted in a 1986
article:

> American aid is geared to the maintenance of that
> modern, sophisticated [military] force rather than to a
> high living standard for Israel's population. . . . This
> situation is cause for considerable concern among cer-
> tain top Israeli officials. They realize that continual
> infusions of American aid prevent Israel from rebuild-
> ing its economy with a proper growth program and the
> establishment of an infrastructure conducive to com-
> petitive industry.[86]

The conclusion Shai Feldman stressed in his interview
was similar to Yitzhak Rabin's assessment quoted earlier.
According to Feldman, "The strategic arguments are the
frosting on the cake, but the moral arguments are the cake
itself."[87]

Conclusion: U.S. Policy-Making

The evidence presented here suggests that the claims made
by Israel's strategic salesman in the United States during
the early and mid-1980s were not only highly exaggerated
but also based on carefully selected facts. Nevertheless, the
relevant U.S. policymakers, whether in the Reagan administration or on Capitol Hill, generally behaved as though
they believed these arguments. What were the implications
of this for U.S. policy-making concerning the Israeli-Syrian
conflict?

Looking first at the situation on Capitol Hill, one
should note that the regular background noise of rhetoric
concerning Israel's "strategic value" to the United States
that emanated from congressional offices during the 1980s
should be considered in most cases to be just that—rheto-

ric. This rhetoric, however, did have consequences for the conduct of the relationship because congressional power of the purse enables it to send powerful messages to the Israelis apart from those sent to Israel by the administration.

One instance where Congress's generosity to Israel significantly affected the conduct of the relationship concerned the Lavi. Dov Zakheim wrote in 1987 that "most senators and congressmen who have followed the issue *are prepared to go along with any decision the Israeli government makes* to scrap the plane."[88] Given the contrast between this permissive attitude toward a clear case of defense contract mismanagement by Israel and the far tougher attitude Congress has traditionally adopted toward lesser cases of mismanagement by the Pentagon, the message to the Lavi's hard-line supporters in Israel (most of them Likudniks) appeared to be clear—the U.S. Congress would continue giving them money for anything they wanted, with few questions asked.[89]

Congress's role, however, in the conduct of foreign policy is constitutionally limited to budgetary matters, to participation in the general public debate over foreign policy, and to overseas troop deployments that threaten to trigger the 1975 War Powers Act. Thus, a more important issue than the degree to which the "strategic Israel" arguments affected Congress was how these arguments affected decision making by the administration.

As indicated above, President Reagan himself and many of his top officials including Secretary of State Haig came into office in 1981 apparently firm in their belief that Israel provided strategic benefits for the United States. For an understanding of how these beliefs affected their conduct of policy in the Israel-Syria theater, it is worth studying the administration's behavior during the June 1982 crisis and the lesser Israel-Syria crises that occurred during their time in office.

One of the lesser crises will be reviewed first—the summer 1981 crisis over Syria's deployment of missiles to the Bekaa. An objective analysis of the crisis would probably have concluded, as most Israeli strategic analysts did, that it was Israel's actions that had initiated the threat to the Red Lines agreements in Lebanon in this case. The Reagan administration failed to point this out and to demand the speedy compliance of both parties with the status quo ante. Instead, the missile crisis was allowed to fester unresolved, with the U.S. administration seemingly unconcerned that Israel had served notice that it no longer felt bound by its commitments under the Red Lines agreements. Thus, although the missile crisis was managed successfully because escalation was prevented in the short term, its management was unsuccessful over the longer term because the United States failed to address the deeper issue of Israel's adherence to the agreements. This failure then encouraged Sharon to launch his full-scale assault on the agreements the following year.

The Reagan administration's policy toward Israel's role in the missile crisis stood in contrast to that of the Carter administration in fall 1977, when the Begin government had tried to transgress an earlier, U.S.-backed limitation on Israel's involvement in Lebanon. On that earlier occasion, the U.S. president sharply warned Begin to get back behind the stated line, and Begin complied.[90] This change in the U.S. attitude toward Israel's transgressions in Lebanon between 1977 and 1981 was entirely consonant with the change in the way key members of the new administration viewed Israel—that is, as a net grantor of, rather than recipient of, strategic benefits under the relationship.

The larger crisis-management challenge to the United States came in June 1982, when Sharon's pursuit of the Big Plan in Lebanon brought the IDF into full-scale confrontation with the Syrian troops in Lebanon. By this time, some key players in the president's immediate entourage, including new national security adviser William Clark, already reportedly entertained some doubt about the strategic value of the link with Israel; and at the higher levels of global escalation threatened by this crisis, the views of the secretary of defense (who was also skeptical of the "strategic Israel" arguments) would presumably carry greater weight than they had in the conduct of the lower-level crisis over the missiles the previous year.

Haig was still secretary of state, however, and he was being urged in public by his former boss Henry Kissinger to use the Israeli action to effect a significant realignment of forces in Lebanon at the expense of Syria, the PLO, and the Soviets as well. The decision making that resulted from an administration that was thus deeply split over how to view Israel's action was understandably confused. (The confusion began to dissipate only after Haig's resignation and the apparent victory of the Clark-Weinberger line.) It should be noted, however, that the confusion in U.S. decision making was evident mainly over the issue of the IDF's actions in Beirut and not over its actions against the Syrian positions in eastern Lebanon. Opposition to the IDF's eastern campaign was apparently unanimous among U.S. decision makers, including the president and Secretary Haig themselves. The U.S. demarche to Israel that it should abide by the cease-fire on the eastern front came, after all, well before Haig's resignation.

Thus, on the one front where Sharon's actions threatened to cause a full-scale Israeli-Syrian war, all his arguments about the strategic services Israel performed for the United States proved insufficient to persuade Haig and Reagan to back his plans. Even these two, for all the credence they apparently gave to the "strategic Israel" rhetoric, showed that their support for Israel's military adventures did not extend to the point where these adventures might embroil the superpowers in another full-scale Middle East war. This fact should give serious pause for thought to any Israeli leader who might plan a future military adventure against Syria.

A number of other factors, however, affected the ability of the administration to restrain the Israelis during the Lebanon crisis. Among these was the sheer size of the military stockpile that the Israelis had acquired by this time, which removed from the United States much of the leverage that it had exerted over Israel in previous Arab-Israeli crises by virtue of its position astride the military resupply spigot. This stockpile size was a direct result of the scale of U.S. military aid to Israel since 1973.

Despite the U.S. loss of resupply leverage, American political support remained a powerful potential lever for U.S. influence over Israel, particularly when allied to the Israeli government's need to maintain a domestic consensus for its actions. This became dramatically clear in September 1982, when the United States was able to force the Israeli government to remove the IDF from West Beirut. The United States accomplished this not by threatening to use force against Israel, nor by threatening to cut or delay military or other aid, but merely by conveying a clear public demarche to the Israelis that they should pull back. This demarche, coming in the context of the domestic Israeli outcry over the refugee camp massacres, was sufficient to force Begin and Sharon to issue the pullback order.

The implication for crisis management of this incident, as well as for the U.S. success in forcing Israeli compliance with the June cease-fire in eastern Lebanon, was clear. Under circumstances in which Israel's domestic consensus was already stretched thin and Israel was not facing a clearly evident threat to its national survival, the United States was able to exert leverage over Israeli decision making through political means alone.[91] In the end the sheer disparity between the strategic weights of the United States and Israel meant that, regardless of the official rhetoric emanating from both sides, Israel was still far more dependent on U.S. goodwill than the United States would ever be on Israel's. Thus, the shift in emphasis that occurred under President Reagan, from viewing the relationship with Israel in primarily moral terms to viewing it primarily through the lens of strategy, still did not give the Israeli leadership carte blanche to launch any adventures throughout the region that might flow from the imagination of a leader such as General Sharon.

The effects of the shift were grave enough, however,

because it was largely under the rubric of Israel's strategic worth to the United States that the United States maintained generous transfers of high-technology arms to Israel during the Reagan years. This policy played a great part in fueling the regional arms race, and it enabled Israel to launch the 1982 expedition into Lebanon that left more than 10,000 dead there, transforming that country's traditional friendship toward the United States into a fund of bitterness whose effects will be felt for many years to come. The Reagan administration's stress on Israel as a strategic asset meanwhile allowed Israel to avoid meeting the challenge of continuing the peace process with its neighbors for which previous presidents had worked assiduously. In the militarily crucial Israel-Syria theater, meanwhile, the Reagan administration made no serious attempt to move the conflict from the battlefield to the negotiating table.

Might there be a change of heart under President Bush? As so often has been the case in U.S.-Israeli relations, it was Israeli analysts who were the first to discuss publicly the fact that the Reagan era's vision of strategic cooperation might no longer — at a time when the Soviet empire was crumbling even in Eastern Europe — correspond with reality. In November 1989 Israeli defense writer Amir Oren told a Washington audience: "From Israel's perspective, the main challenge to strategic cooperation is the erosion of the anti-Soviet rationale that originally energized U.S. policymakers to pursue the [strategic] relationship."[92] That same month, Ze'ev Schiff wrote that if the Israelis did not adapt themselves to the new changes in the global political environment, "the time might come when we ask what is the new basis for the strategic cooperation between us and the United States. We might find that the rug has been pulled out from under our feet."[93] Schiff also revealed in this article that a year earlier, U.S. participants in the biannual meetings of the JPMG had concluded that merely annual meetings would thenceforth be sufficient. The Israeli side was reportedly able to prevent this move, which they considered a downgrading of the entire collaboration.

But the combination of signals from many participants in the Bush administration's Middle East policy-making, including the Pentagon officials interviewed for the present research as well as President Bush himself and Secretary of State James Baker, indicated clearly that sooner or later the tumultuous changes in world politics must affect the U.S.-Israeli relationship.[94]

4

The Soviet-Syrian Relationship

In which direction was leverage influenced in the Soviet-Syrian relationship during the period under study? Was the Soviet dog able to wag the Syrian tail at will, as implied by some analysts?[1] Or did the nature of the relationship between the two allow the Syrian tail to wag the Soviet dog?

In fact, as the following analysis indicates, there was a noticeable dynamism in the relationship between these two actors during the years between 1978 and 1989. This conclusion accords with those reached by some other careful analysts of this topic, such as Efraim Karsh or John Hannah. In his 1988 study, Karsh concluded that the Soviet-Syrian relationship "should be portrayed in terms of a mutually beneficial *strategic interdependence* between two allies: a relationship favoring each partner in accordance with the vicissitudes in regional and global affairs."[2] Karsh judged that, in the aftermath of the 1973 Middle East war, Syria gained "real leverage" over the Soviets, but he added: "Fortunately for Moscow, this imbalance has gradually disappeared since 1977."[3] John Hannah, in a review of the evidence available by the middle of 1989, concluded:

Whereas in the past, the numerous conflicts of interest that arose between the two countries generally seemed to result in the Syrian tail wagging the Soviet dog for higher levels of arms and support for Damascus' confrontational policies, Gorbachev seems to be trying to establish the principle that Soviet actions will be dictated more by Russian interests than Syrian bellicosity.[4]

To gauge the validity of these judgments for the purposes of this study, this chapter first recapitulates some of the most important turning points in the Soviet-Syrian relationship since the early 1970s and then evaluates some of the different interests that the Soviets appear to have been pursuing through the relationship. (The interests the Syrians were pursuing through the link were addressed in chapter 2.) This analysis will then be used in chapter 5 to assess the prospects for successful crisis management or conflict resolution in the years ahead.

Key Developments in Soviet-Syrian Relations

By the time Israel and Egypt concluded the Camp David accords in 1978, the relationship with the Soviet Union had become a constant, though never problem-free, feature of Syrian politics. In 1944 the Soviet Union had been the first great power to recognize independent Syria (as, four years later, it was among the first to recognize Israel). In 1956 the Syrians concluded their first arms agreement with the Soviets. The arms-supply relationship continued during the years that followed despite the frequent changes of regime that plagued Syria through 1970. It survived both Syria's defeat in the 1967 Middle East war and the 1970 seizure of power by Hafiz al-Asad. Asad was regarded at that time with some suspicion in Moscow because of his perceived rightist preferences regarding domestic policy, although Soviet analysts were reassured that his caution regarding strategic affairs promised them more predictability in the Arab-Israeli theater than had the more impetuous strategic

policies of his predecessors.[5] This dichotomy in the way
the Soviets judged different parts of Asad's policy (which
represented a fairly accurate assessment of his preferences)
would continue to pose a dilemma for Soviet policymakers
throughout Asad's lengthy rule in Syria—until the Soviets
unequivocally began to place more importance on the strategic stability of the region than on the prospects for enhancing the socialist orientation of the Syrian regime.

Until 1972 the Soviets' relationship with Syria was always subordinate to that with Egypt. That year, in the
aftermath of President Anwar Sadat's ouster of Soviet military advisers, the Soviets upgraded their relationship with
Asad. Soviet arms supplies during 1972–1973 then allowed
Syria (as they did Egypt) to launch the October 1973 offensive against Israel.[6]

After the 1973 war, Asad launched an opening toward
the United States that caused the Soviets increasing concern. They turned a blind eye to the fact that he (as had
Sadat before him) turned to unilateral U.S. mediation to
conclude a disengagement agreement with Israel because
they considered this to accord with their own interests in
stabilizing the military situation in the region. Then, in
1976 a coalition between Lebanese leftists and PLO forces
based in Lebanon threatened to overthrow the pro-Western, Maronite-dominated regime in Beirut. Asad sent his
forces into the country to buttress the existing regime—
against the express advice of the Soviets, who had good
relations with the Lebanese leftists and the PLO, but with
the support of the Americans. When Syria subsequently
received small amounts of U.S. economic aid, the Soviets
grew fearful that Asad might follow Sadat along the path
of exchanging his relationship with them for a more seduc-
tive link with Washington.

In the period of strain that ensued, lasting from the
spring of 1976 until the end of 1977, many long-standing
differences between the two sides began to be aired publicly
for the first time. These differences included disagreements
over such diplomatic issues as the continuing Syrian presence in Lebanon; Asad's failure to rise above his rivalry

with the regime in Iraq, another important Soviet ally in the region; and his reluctance to grant the recognition of Israel that Moscow understood must be a part of any resumption of the Arab-Israeli peace process. Long-standing disagreements over ideological and social issues were also aired at this time (see below).

During the latter half of 1977, the new administration in Washington took two different steps in its Middle East policy that had a direct effect on the Soviets' relations with Syria. The first of these was the short-lived effort, embodied in the U.S.-Soviet joint communiqué of October 1977, to include the Soviets in the Middle East peace process.[7] This move threatened to introduce some strain into the Soviet-Syrian relationship because in any resumed peace process the Soviets might have to lean quite hard on the Syrians to contribute constructively to the negotiations. Within days, however, the United States had backed away decisively from the cooperative approach to the Middle East, and over the weeks that followed it lent its backing to Sadat's peace initiative with Israel.

This second U.S. move had a strong impact on the Soviet-Syrian relationship because the Sadat initiative and the Camp David accords that resulted from it were viewed as extremely threatening by Soviets and Syrians alike. For the Soviets, the unilateral U.S. sponsorship of the accords seemed to deny them any diplomatic role in a sensitive part of the world close to their own borders. They saw the Multinational Force and Observers (MFO) that deployed to Sinai under the accords, with its contingents coming from the United States and other Western nations, as an integral part of NATO war planning. The entire situation looked to Moscow as though it were an integral part of the sinister new American policy of anti-Soviet containment that their analysts were later to describe as "neoglobalism."[8] The effect of the Sadat initiative and the resulting Camp David accords on Soviet-Syrian relations was thus to throw both parties defensively into each other's arms, notwithstanding their mutual strong reservations.

In December 1977 the Soviets backed Syria's creation

of the anti-Egyptian Steadfastness and Confrontation Front by sending increased arms shipments to its members. They also strongly urged the Syrians to patch up their rivalry with Iraq, but by July 1979, as has been seen, these conciliation efforts clearly had come to naught.

In October 1980 a vulnerable and isolated Syria finally acceded to longtime Soviet requests to conclude a formal Treaty of Friendship and Cooperation.[9] The Soviets went to some lengths to stress the restricted nature of the commitments that they had given Syria under the treaty; General-Secretary Leonid Brezhnev stated, "This is a treaty in the name of peace, not in the name of war."[10] Soviet officials later noted that its provisions did not include any Soviet commitment to support Syrian troop deployments outside Syria.[11] That this interpretation seemed valid was indicated when Moscow responded with disapproval when Asad dispatched tank units to his border with Jordan the following month.

The interpretation of the treaty's provisions as not including any commitment to the support of Syrian military units deployed outside Syria was also proven valid — at least through the fall of 1982 — by Moscow's attitude to the unfolding Syrian-Israeli confrontations in Lebanon. Shortly after the crisis over Syria's deployment of missiles to the Bekaa in May 1981, the Soviet ambassador in Lebanon stressed that "the recent developments are unrelated to the Soviet-Syrian treaty."[12] According to Efraim Karsh, on this occasion the Soviet Union signaled "its clear interest in containing the crisis."[13]

Israel's June 1982 invasion of Lebanon came at a difficult time for the rulers in Moscow. They were deeply embroiled in the power struggles accompanying Brezhnev's lengthy physical decline and, according to one ranking Soviet researcher, had just begun to feel the effects of their policy failure in Afghanistan. This researcher stressed that the Soviet rulers were surprised by the extent of the Israeli action because they had assumed that the Red Lines regime in Lebanon was still fundamentally stable. Another analyst, the well-connected Igor Belyayev, referred in a 1988 interview to the possibility of Syrian collusion with Israel during the war. Belyayev declined to elaborate further on this point. (This type of collusion theory has been most systematically developed by Palestinian nationalists, with whom Belyayev has enjoyed long, and apparently friendly, contacts.)[14] If the suspicion that Belyayev voiced in 1988 had been seriously entertained by Soviet decision makers in 1982, it would have implied a significant breakdown of trust between them and President Asad during that crucial period. For his part, the Foreign Ministry's Gennady Terasov recalled that his government had sent at least one direct message to Israeli Premier Begin during the fighting, although he offered no further details.[15] Even if this recollection were to be proven true, however, it would do little to counter the overall assessment of Soviet policies during the fighting as having been cautious, muted, and essentially reactive.

In the aftermath of Israel's destruction of the Bekaa SAMs, Brezhnev was able (as noted in chapter 2) to react by sending a warning letter to U.S. President Reagan. Then, after the cease-fire took hold on the Israeli-Syrian sector, Asad took advantage of the breathing space it provided to make his emergency visit to Moscow. But by the end of the summer it was clear that the Soviets had suffered a major loss of prestige in the Middle East because of their apparent passivity over the Lebanon crisis, as well as the apparent inferiority of their weaponry as demonstrated there. The United States emerged as the sole outside broker of the cease-fire arrangement in Beirut, and in September 1982 it proposed a new Middle East peace plan under unilateral U.S. sponsorship. When U.S. and West European troops deployed to Lebanon under the auspices of MNF-2, the combination of NATO forces and unilateral U.S. peace proposals seemed to the Soviets like a threatening replay of Camp David. The Syrians also felt extremely threatened by their apparent exclusion from the U.S. peace plan, as well as by the MNF-2 deployment. The result was that, as had occurred four years earlier, the U.S. moves threw the Soviets and Syrians back into a defensive alliance.

This time, the Soviet and Syrian efforts to counter U.S. plans for the region (both those the United States may actually have harbored and those imputed to them) were much more successful than earlier efforts against Camp David. The Soviets stabilized Syria's strategic position by deploying SAM-5 air-defense missiles there in January 1983, while the Syrians and their Lebanese allies went in for the kill against the U.S. position in Lebanon. In the winter of 1983–1984, U.S. naval and ground forces in the Lebanon area came dangerously close to engaging not only the local pro-Syrian fighting groups but also Syrian regular army positions in which Soviet advisers were quite possibly present. One well-positioned Soviet expert has recalled that, especially at a time when the conflict was heating up in Afghanistan, the Soviet rulers were extremely unwilling to be dragged into an additional confrontation elsewhere.[16] As the political and military pressure on the U.S. position in Lebanon mounted that winter, however, their counterparts in Washington decisively signaled that maintaining their increasingly exposed position was not worth the risks involved. In February 1984 the United States decided to withdraw, and MNF-2 was disbanded.

The broader Arab-Israeli peace plan that the United States had proposed in 1982 continued to stumble along as U.S. policy after February 1984. By early 1986, however, Jordan's King Hussein – a key player in the U.S. plan – had declared that he could not enter a peace process without Soviet and Syrian support and entered a new political alliance with Damascus. This dealt the final, fatal blow to the U.S. plan.

Acting in concert, the Soviets and Syrians were thus able to achieve what both sides considered significant victories in the Middle East between fall 1982 and 1986. These victories were all the more significant because they were won amid political instability in Damascus, repeated leadership transitions in Moscow, and extreme stress in the bilateral superpower relationship.

The Soviet-Syrian victories of 1982 through 1986 were even more surprising because they were registered while the existing distrust between the two sides continued unabated over many of their other differences. The Soviets were generally appalled by the bitter military and political campaign that Asad waged against the mainstream PLO in the years after 1982. After all, PLO Chairman Yasir Arafat, along with Asad, played a key role in Soviet plans to find a way into any future Middle East peace process. (The Soviets, however, did not trust Arafat's professions of loyalty to their common goals any more than they did Asad's. In 1985, when it looked as though Arafat might find a way to join negotiations with Israel held under unilateral U.S. sponsorship, the Soviets exerted pressure inside the PLO alongside the Syrians—but notably not in alliance with them—in an attempt to stop him. In 1986, partly as a result of these pressures, that ill-fated subsection of the peace process reached a dead end.)[17]

At the military level, meanwhile, the Soviets may have been willing, in the years after 1982, to stabilize Asad's situation by helping him to achieve an unprecedented military buildup for his country. They remained adamantly opposed, however, to risking being dragged into the kind of Arab-Israeli confrontation likely to result if he should ever actually achieve his stated goal of "strategic parity" with Israel. This was evident from, among other things, the record of Soviet arms transfers to Syria. John Hannah has calculated that between 1985 and 1989 the Soviets annually delivered an average of $1.3 billion worth of weapons to Syria, compared with an annual rate of transfers valued at $2.9 billion in the period 1980–1984.[18]

For their part, the Syrians had little alternative but to chafe under these restrictions. Meanwhile, they grew increasingly uneasy at the Soviets' accelerating efforts to reach out diplomatically to a spectrum of Arab states and even (albeit more tentatively) to Israel. This history of continuing differences set the stage for the bombshell of April 1987, when Gorbachev invited Asad to Moscow, only to berate him in full public view at a state dinner for the unrealistic nature of his policy toward Israel (see chapter 2).

In Damascus, the Gorbachev speech seemed to provoke some rapid reconsideration of whether the regime could continue to take Soviet diplomatic and military support for granted. Shortly after Asad left the Soviet Union, he withdrew his ambassador from Moscow in a move that seemed to signal discontent. A new ambassador was not sent back there until more than a year later.[19] On the Soviet side, meanwhile, one of the officials involved in drafting Gorbachev's speech later explained that the Soviet leader's aim had been "to get out of the rut of hoping that further military shipments would solve our problems with the Arabs." The official said that the Soviets hoped, with the speech, to stress the shift from military to political means of waging the Arab-Israeli struggle. He commented that the Syrians' ideal of strategic parity was "just another codeword for the arms race" and asked, "Anyway, how can we ever measure it?" Other analysts in Moscow made some fairly harsh judgments about the Syrians' ability to use effectively the military hardware they already had.[20]

Despite the reservations that were voiced increasingly openly in Moscow in the late 1980s concerning the value of the relationship with Syria, there still seemed – at least through the end of 1989 – to be a consensus among policymakers there that the relationship was worth retaining, albeit in a possibly modified form. In November 1989 the Soviet ambassador in Damascus, Alexander Zotov, reportedly said that his country's efforts to meet Syria's future military needs would consider Syria's "ability to pay" and observe the principle of "reasonable defensive sufficiency."[21] After these comments were published, Zotov called a press conference to argue that his remarks had been quoted out of context. In an interview with a Kuwaiti newspaper at the beginning of 1990, however, Deputy Foreign Minister Vladimir Polyakov echoed many of the same points Zotov had made. Polyakov specifically noted that "Syria is our closest ally in the region." But he also devoted a considerable proportion of the interview to arguing that

> the Arabs must search for the quickest and best ways to settle the Middle East conflict, because if the conflict continues, tension in the region will increase and military arsenals will continue to be built up. . . .
> So far, the conflict in the region has not been resolved and certain Arab states are, regrettably, in a state of belligerence, and we take this matter into consideration. Therefore we use the theory of reasonable defense sufficiency. This theory must be used by all states and in all regions in the world.[22]

Clearly, therefore, the Soviets were undertaking a serious reappraisal of their commitments to Syria. This reappraisal was parallel to, though not necessarily of the same order as, the review they were making and remaking toward other allies such as those in Eastern Europe during the last tumultuous months of 1989. To explore the possible dimensions of the reappraisal toward Syria, it is necessary to examine the different kinds of interests the Soviets had been pursuing in their relationship with Syria throughout the period under study, as well as the changes these interests had already sustained in the mold-breaking first five years of the Gorbachev era.

Ideological Considerations

By 1978, Soviet policymakers had few illusions left about sharing much ideological affinity with the regime in Syria. Elizabeth Kridl Valkenier has dated to "about 1980" a move by Soviet theoreticians to reduce expectations concerning the pro-Soviet potential of Third World anti-imperialist movement.[23] With respect, however, to the theoretical category to which Soviet analysis assigned the Asad regime in Syria—that of "socialist orientation"—there is evidence that a more pessimistic judgment of the "revolutionary" potential of these states had been formulated at authoritative levels within the Communist Party of the Soviet Union (CPSU) bureaucracy some years prior to 1980.

Consider, for example, the work of Karen Brutents, who by 1976 had become a deputy chief of the CPSU International Department. As early as 1973, Brutents was writing that some of the rulers of socialist-oriented states "are inclined to maneuver between the two systems on the world arena."[24] Brutents noted the anti-imperialist role of the state economic sector in some of the more developed Third World countries, citing Syria as one named example. Immediately after this accolade, however, he referred to "instances of corruption and self-enrichment" by officials in this sector and noted:

> This stratum, completely bourgeoisified in its psychology, gives itself over to parasitic consumption, but is as a rule not strong enough to use its illegally gotten wealth as a basis for major or often even for medium enterprise. . . . They are quite capable of acting as the potential basis for a pro-bourgeois policy.[25]

In a book published in 1979, Brutents included some biting criticism of the role of the "bureaucratic bourgeoisie" in some of the socialist-oriented countries, though this time he did not specifically mention Syria. Then, when he revised this book for an English edition that went to press in 1983, he noted in a new addition to the work that the Syrian Communist Party (SCP) had joined the Ba'thists in the Patriotic National Front, which nominally controlled the Syrian government, but he added: "The Syrian Communists do not close their eyes to shortcomings in the front's activities and to the negative sides of the Ba'th Party's approach to cooperation with the Communists."[26]

By virtue of his International Department position, Brutents was already one of the most influential Soviet theoreticians on these subjects. His influence on policy-making probably further increased in the early years of the Gorbachev era, despite some reorganizations of the CPSU's work on foreign affairs.[27] In an interview in July 1988, Brutents claimed with some justification that he had long been less optimistic than other Soviet analysts concerning the revolutionary potential of socialist-oriented states. He noted that in his theoretical work he had stressed the problems encountered by the countries with "socialist orientation," emphasizing factors such as the objective immaturity of the socioeconomic base in these countries and the difficulties they faced in pursuing an anti-imperialist path within the world capitalist market system. Commenting on the contribution of ideological analysis to the formulation of Soviet foreign policy, this professional ideologist wryly advocated that "one should restrain one's ideological passions, because you can't rebuild everything at once!"[28]

A survey of the Soviet Union's Middle East policy during the decade of the present study would indicate that policymakers generally seemed to share Brutents's skepticism concerning the "socialist" or "anti-imperialist" rhetoric of such regimes as Syria's. And other conclusions of Brutents's work, such as his emphasis on the relative stability of the capitalist regimes in the Third World and the potential value to the Soviets of building relations with such states, were clearly shared by policymakers on Middle Eastern issues beginning in the early 1980s. Throughout the post-Brezhnev period, the Soviets were working hard and with some success on upgrading their ties with conservative states such as Jordan, the Gulf monarchies, and even that repository of numerous dashed Soviet hopes and Syrian jealousies – Egypt.

Under Gorbachev, this twin process of spreading the Soviet bets in the Middle East and not being impressed by the rhetoric of nominally socialist states like Syria further accelerated. The contribution to Middle East policy of an official Soviet ideology that was itself in a state of great flux thus seemed to be only further decreased. It redounded to the advantage of the role played by a new, more frankly expressed realpolitik. In late 1987 Yevgeniy Primakov (who was flourishing professionally under Gorbachev even more than was Brutents) stated bluntly that the Soviet Union had "no class interests in the Middle East, only state interest."[29] This utterance was in line with the point of view expressed by Foreign Minister Shevardnadze at a gathering of ministry personnel in Moscow in July 1988. According to a *Pravda* report, Shevardnadze told the meeting that "the struggle between two opposing systems is no longer a determining tendency of the present-day era."[30]

By the end of 1989 the ideological edifice that Soviet theoreticians had so painstakingly constructed for the international affairs of the Brezhnev era was clearly in ruins. With the Soviet empire crumbling in Eastern Europe, the Baltic States, and the Caucasus, the fine ideological distinctions that Brezhnev-era theoreticians had sought to draw between states of socialist or capitalist orientation in the Third World rapidly became irrelevant.

All that remained was the need to evaluate the degree to which the ideological interest of spreading world socialism or communism had affected Soviet policy during the period before the radical changes of the Gorbachev era. In the case of the relationship with Syria, these types of interests had never had a very strong impact on Soviet policy during the post–Camp David period. Rather, it was strategic and global political interests that had driven the Soviets' continuing relationship with Asad. How were these other types of interest defined in the years from 1978 to 1989, and how did changes in the way the Soviets viewed them affect their relationship with Syria?

Military-Strategic Considerations

Since the dawn of the atomic age, the highest national-security concern of the Soviet Union's rulers has been with planning to survive or (later) to prevent global nuclear warfare. Beginning in the late 1950s, global nuclear considerations have had a direct bearing on their view of the eastern Mediterranean region inhabited by Syria and Israel. Syria has, in addition, contributed to Soviet planning for conventional war-fighting. In the systematic way the Soviet leaders think about strategic affairs, however, considerations of conventional war-planning are less important than nuclear considerations; so these latter will be addressed first.

The eastern Mediterranean has impinged on Soviet nuclear planning in two major ways. First, Soviet planners have at some stages considered it necessary to deny the Americans the option of maintaining in the eastern Mediterranean a viable second-strike nuclear capability against the Soviet Union's southern industrial heartland. Therefore, even in peacetime the Soviets had to maintain a permanent, sea-based counter to the American submarine-based nuclear force there; this, in turn, necessitated access to shore-based naval support facilities. After being ousted from Yugoslavia and Albania, it was thus with some relief that in 1967 the Soviet Mediterranean squadron gained access to Egyptian ports.[31]

Naval strategist Michael MccGwire has convincingly demonstrated, however, that Soviet military doctrine underwent fundamental change at the end of the 1960s. One consequence of this change, as he saw it, was that the Soviets no longer considered it necessary to maintain a permanent counter to the U.S. submarine presence in the eastern Mediterranean.[32] Thus, when the Egyptians started curtailing Soviet access to their naval facilities in 1972, this access was no longer the important requirement for the Soviets that it had been five years earlier. And by the late 1970s and 1980s, although the Soviet Mediterranean squadron continued to use shore-based naval facilities in Syria and elsewhere, they were no longer so vitally dependent on the goodwill of these littoral countries as they had previously considered themselves to be on Egypt.

The second way in which the eastern Mediterranean has impinged on Soviet global nuclear planning is through the potential of the chronically festering Arab-Israeli dispute to draw the superpowers into a global confrontation of possibly nuclear proportions. One of the Soviet writers who has referred most frequently to this possibility is Yevgeniy Primakov. It is interesting to chart, for key points during the decade under study, the terms in which he referred to the explosive potential of the Arab-Israeli dispute. His writings, indeed, provide a fairly authoritative window through which one can view a Soviet calculus that has changed according to more general Soviet assessments of the nature of the relationship with the United States.

In 1978, in his book-length work on the region, Primakov provided a detailed expression of his views of American strategic interests in the Middle East. He wrote that at the global level, "at the beginning of the 1970s the leaders of the United States finally had to admit that there was a military and strategic equilibrium between their country and the USSR." But his view, in that first period of détente, was not entirely rosy. He referred to a "contradictory situation, when, on the one hand, signs of realism have become manifest in U.S. policy and, on the other, ultra-imperialist reactionaries are influencing American foreign-policy decisions."[33] He spelled out that détente "will most likely not be a simple process at all," and concluded that, even in a situation of détente, "the United States sees the Middle East as an important link in the global confrontation with the USSR."[34] In the concluding chapter of this work, Primakov still seemed cautiously optimistic. He noted, however, that "the development and realisation of détente and making détente irreversible now depend to a large degree on removing sources of international tension. One of these and one of the most dangerous, is the Middle East."[35]

In 1985, Primakov was more clearly alarmed at the explosive potential of the Arab-Israeli conflict. In a book published that year, he dwelt at some length on what he considered U.S.-Israeli collusion during Israel's invasion of Lebanon in 1982 and on the strategic implications of this link. In the conclusion of this book, he wrote:

During the Reagan Presidency American policy in the Middle East to a degree ever greater than before became based indeed on striving for the "universalization" of the struggle against the Soviet Union by taking it from the global to the regional level. This has intensified tension in the world and has made the development of the international situation even more dangerous.[36]

In 1988 Primakov was still listing the explosive potential of the Arab-Israeli conflict at the head of this list of Soviet concerns in the region. He wrote that "the Middle East occupies a special place in the hierarchy of Soviet foreign policy interests. . . . Sharp conflict, periodically escalating to crisis level, has existed in the Middle East for several decades, causing military and political concern in the Soviet Union."[37] He now seemed more hopeful than he had been in 1985, however, that as a result of the easing of tensions between his country and the United States it might be possible to negotiate an end to the Arab-Israeli conflict. He offered a fairly detailed scenario for these negotiations, judging that such a scenario "might be possible" and saying that the influence of both the Soviet Union and the United States would be essential for such an effort to succeed. But he still warned that, if such an approach were not followed, "the Middle East will move toward a catastrophe on a scale difficult to predict, bringing disasters not only to Arabs and Israelis, but to the entire international community as well."[38]

Other analysts and policymakers interviewed in Moscow in 1988 agreed with this conclusion. Some of them believed that although there was now greater understanding between the two superpowers concerning the Middle East, at the same time each had less control than hitherto over the actions of its local partners there. One member of this group, Foreign Ministry official Gennady Terasov, ascribed the lessening of the superpowers' control in part to the acquisition by local powers of ballistic missiles "that they could launch at any time."[39]

Beginning in 1985, Soviet analysts wrote increasingly explicit descriptions of Israel's nuclear weapons capabilities.[40] Toward the end of the decade, they were identifying a clear link between the nuclear and missile capabilities of local parties to regional conflicts, on the one hand, and the potential for global instability, on the other. One such writer, V. Kuznetsov, spelled out in a December 1989 article in *Pravda* that Israel was at the top of Soviet concerns in this regard. He noted that the Jericho-2 missile tested by Israel in 1987 had the capability of striking "even at southern Soviet cities" and judged that the rocket system used to put the Israeli satellite into orbit in 1988 "is classed as an ICBM and can be adapted to deliver a nuclear warhead."[41] Kuznetsov also referred to Israel's secret nuclear installation in the Negev, along with similar Pakistani and South African facilities, adding that "it is in precisely these complexes that preparations are being made to cross the 'nuclear threshold.' Perhaps it has already been crossed in some places."[42] He commented:

> When we speak of a "major" war, it usually occurs to us that it might flare up between the USSR and the United States. Or in Europe. But the threat of such a conflict has now been set aside and is becoming less likely. On the other hand, there are ever-increasing grounds for concern that the irremediable might happen in the "third world."[43]

Kuznetsov's article clearly indicated that, even though the major bilateral tensions with the United States had abated by 1989, there was still reason for those in the Soviet Union charged with formulating nuclear strategy to follow developments in the Arab-Israeli theater with close concern. In the field of planning for conventional warfare, meanwhile, the Arab-Israeli arena had for decades provided the Soviets with valuable lessons about the capabilities of many types of Western weaponry that their forces would encounter in an engagement against NATO forces in Europe. In the period under study, there is considerable evidence that during the 1982 fighting in Lebanon, the lessons the Soviets learned were of some value to them.[44] The director of the Military History Institute in the Soviet Ministry of Defense, Colonel-General Dmitri Volkogonov, admitted in a 1988 interview that this had been the case, although he declined to elaborate beyond noting that the Soviets had learned new lessons about combat readiness.[45]

The Soviets have historically been more fearful than their Washington counterparts of the danger of even limited conventional conflicts in the Third World escalating into worldwide confrontations. It is thus probably incorrect to argue, as some in the West have done, that Soviet central planners have actually welcomed such conflicts as test-beds for their conventional weaponry. This is not to say that when such lessons are provided, as in 1982, that Soviet analysts are not ready and eager to absorb them. But it does imply that, where global escalation is seen as a real risk, the Soviets would try to restrain their Third World allies from engaging against Western-backed forces — unless there were overriding considerations of Soviet global strategic planning at stake. (MccGwire has indicated that this might have been true in the Arab-Israeli conflict of 1967.)[46] Beginning in the early 1970s, however, there was no such overriding concern on the Soviet side; and the posture that the Soviets maintained toward the prospect of an Arab-Israeli war during the period of the present study is aptly summed up by Efraim Karsh's sobriquet, "the cautious bear."[47]

In light of the above, how are we to judge the Soviet decision to aid the Syrians in the force buildup that was inaugurated in late 1982 with the acquisition of the SAM-5s? The United States did not have evidence of the Syrian SAM-5 deployment until early 1983, but the Soviet decision to supply the SAMs had clearly, given the lead time involved, been made some weeks earlier. Patrick Seale implied that this decision had been made during Asad's visit to Moscow for Brezhnev's funeral in the middle of Novem-

ber 1982, while U.S. analyst Francis Fukuyama believed that it must have been made in September or October.[48] This latter date would have rendered the decision
more directly a reaction to the Reagan peace plan and the
MNF-2 deployment. Soviet analysts interviewed in 1988
did not give a firm date for the SAM-5 decision. But one of
them judged that it had been taken "in a timely and effective fashion."[49]

The Soviet decision to send the SAM-5s (and, subsequently, the SS-21s) to Syria raised the Soviet stakes in
the still-simmering Israeli-Syrian conflict both by raising
the level of overt commitment to Syria and by exposing
the Soviet air-defense crews who accompanied them to a
direct risk of engagement. (The Soviet crews started to be
withdrawn within the next two to three years, as Syrians
were trained to replace them.) Fukuyama has described the
Soviet decision on the SAMs as "highly risky," primarily
for the second of these reasons.[50] Melvin Goodman, however, has challenged the view that this was an example of
Soviet risk-taking on the grounds that, in view of the Soviets' need to strengthen their credibility in the region at that
time, it would have been more risky for them not to have
supplied the SAM-5s to Syria.[51]

In a 1988 interview in Moscow, USA Institute analyst
Viktor Kremenyuk referred to the SAM-5 deployment as
having had a stabilizing effect. He considered the Soviet
decision to send the missiles to Syria an example of the
helpful type of step a superpower could take to lengthen
the time available to decision makers during future crises
and mitigate the hair-trigger aspect of modern warfare.
Looking back with the benefit of hindsight, Kremenyuk
judged that in 1982, the Soviets had actually overplayed
the threat stemming from the MNF-2 deployment. The
main threat at that time had stemmed instead, he asserted,
from the proximity of U.S. and Soviet troops in the region.
He admitted that this proximity had caused "some
tension." Nevertheless, he judged that "both sides were
cautious."[52]

Military-History Institute chief Volkogonov judged that, although political relations between the superpowers were extremely strained in the 1982–1983 period, "there still was a political mechanism that prevented direct great power conflict" in the Arab-Israeli theater. According to Volkogonov, neither superpower sought a total victory for one of the local parties over the other at that time. He and other senior Soviet analysts interviewed noted that the types of arms shipped to Syria did not at any stage in the 1980s allow the Syrians to plan for a surprise offensive against Israel.[53]

Whatever the risks involved in their decisions of late 1982 to stabilize Syria's military position, the Soviets were able thereby to succeed in countering the Reagan plan and the MNF-2 deployment. At a time when the Soviet leaders considered themselves to be in a state of tension with the United States, these were judged to be worthwhile achievements. Over the years that followed, however, the Soviet strategic calculus concerning the region underwent some change. This change was driven primarily by the emergence of post-Brezhnev "new thinking" on the need to ease global tensions, starting with the bilateral relationship with Washington. With regard to Soviet policies in the Israel-Syria theater, the extent of this change can be gauged by reference to a number of new Soviet policies: the record of decreasing Soviet arms deliveries to Syria beginning in 1985; Gorbachev's willingness to deliver public strictures to President Asad in 1987 to the effect that the military instrument had become discredited in the Arab-Israeli theater; and the new relationship that was cautiously built with Israel from 1987 on. The kinds of military service the Syrians had been able to perform in 1982–1984 thus seemed rapidly, from the middle of the decade, to lose much of their value to the Soviets. By the end of the decade, official Soviet commentaries on the Arab-Israeli situation made little or no reference to the Soviet-Syrian "victories" that had been so highly praised in 1984.

Volkogonov's assessment in 1988 was that "local wars

in the Middle East are impossible to win. Therefore it is time for the local powers to draw the same conclusions that the superpowers have concerning nuclear war—namely that there can be no winner for these wars."[54] If, as seems likely, this official military historian's view reflected that of the Soviet defense establishment, then the Syrians could expect no help from the Soviets if they should try to regain their occupied territories in the Golan through the use of military force. Concerning Lebanon, although the Soviets and the United States appeared to agree from 1988 on that Syria should have a preponderance, but not a monopoly, of influence over whichever regime might emerge in Beirut, both superpowers had also clearly indicated that they no longer considered Lebanon the important global battlefield that it had been in the early 1980s. The battlefield military interests the Soviets were pursuing in their relationship with Syria had thus withered back to a bare minimum, vastly overshadowed in the Arab-Israeli region by the need to contain or deter the threat posed to global stability by regional states' burgeoning missile and nuclear capabilities.

What was not clear at the end of the 1980s was whether or to what extent the Soviets looked to Syria to help handle this threat. The Soviets' performance at the Paris chemical weapons conference in January 1989, when they opposed Arab efforts to link the chemical weapons issue with the question of nuclear proliferation, would seem to indicate that they would not be happy counting on Syria to "deter" any Israeli use of nuclear weapons by countering with a threat of chemical attack.

Global Political Considerations

Beginning in the mid-1980s, the military component of the Soviets' relationship with Syria was losing much of its value. Soviet analysts and policymakers still continued to insist, however, until the very last months of the decade, that the relationship retained considerable political significance. This attitude seemed to derive from two principal sources — the firm opposition of the Asad regime to the conclusion of the same kind of *pax Americana* to the Arab-Israeli conflict that the Soviets themselves had also long opposed and the need to safeguard the political investment that had already been sunk into the relationship. (This latter consideration can best be summed up under the general political rubric of "the credibility of Soviet commitments.")

Opposition to U.S. unilateralism in Arab-Israeli peacemaking had been a constant of Soviet policy in the region until nearly the end of the decade under study. During several key periods, when the possibility of such American success seemed particularly worrisome to the Soviets, the Syrians played a large part in preventing or limiting that success. This situation had pertained in 1978, when Syrian opposition to Camp David helped to prevent other significant Arab states from joining Egypt in the U.S.-sponsored peace process. It was also true of 1982, when Syria's opposition helped to kill the Reagan plan; and it was true once again in 1985, when Syria helped to block negotiations that were tentatively being explored between the United States, Israel, and a putative Jordanian-PLO team.

Several reasons, however, suggest that the lasting value of the "service" the Syrians performed for the Soviets in this regard should not be exaggerated. First, the motivation for the Syrians' behavior on an issue of core importance to them was never primarily to provide a service to the Soviets but rather was dictated by their own compelling national security reasons. Thus, the Syrian attitude toward an American peace initiative could be expected to be different if they were offered a tangible role. As the Soviets knew from their experience with Asad in the mid-1970s, he harbored no deep-seated opposition to U.S. policies as such. In that earlier period, he had appeared quite willing to go against what the Soviets considered to be their interests as he worked with, rather than against, the Americans in Lebanon. (In 1988 he was working with the Americans in Lebanon once again. On this latter occasion, however, his decision to do so won support, not opposition, from the Soviets.)

A second reason not to exaggerate the political service Asad performed in blocking a *pax Americana* in the region is that he was never the only, or on some occasions even the strongest, force that attempted to do so. Jordan, the PLO, Iraq, and Saudi Arabia all decided against joining the Camp David process in 1978 for their own reasons. In 1982 the depth of Asad's opposition to the Reagan peace plan was at least matched, if not surpassed, by that of Israel's Likud Bloc leaders. And in 1985 significant bodies of opinion within the PLO, the United States, and Israel were all working against what was still only a tentative peace move.

Throughout the latter years of the 1980s, one of the most promising aspects for the Soviets of their developing rapprochement with Egypt and the more tentative contacts they developed with political forces in Israel was the increasing commitment of these other actors to the idea that further Arab-Israeli peace moves required active Soviet participation. Given that these parties could hope to be far more effective than Syria in persuading Washington to permit a Soviet role, they were emerging in these years as potentially more valuable regional partners for the Soviets at the political level than were the Syrians.

Meanwhile, Asad's tendency to become mired in deep rivalries with other Arab states and parties had always caused major problems for the Soviets as they attempted to improve or maintain their relations with these parties. We have noted the degree to which this applied to Iraq and the PLO; Syria's continuing hostility to Egypt also caused increasing difficulties for the Soviets as they tried to improve their relations with Cairo beginning in 1983. In their private and public commentaries about Syria, the Soviets always laid pointed stress on the need for "Arab unity." In December 1989, when the Egyptians and Syrians finally decided to restore the diplomatic relations that had been severed 12 years earlier, the Soviets were among the first external powers to welcome the move.[55] But Syria remained in a state of political rivalry bordering on outright hostility with both Iraq and the PLO.

A third and more important reason not to exaggerate the Syrians' service to the Soviets in blocking a *pax Americana* was that the Americans' insistence on brokering such a unilaterally sponsored peace, and the Soviets' attitude toward their doing so, had both shifted appreciably by the end of the 1980s. Beginning in 1987, the United States was expressing a readiness to grant the Soviets some type of role in any final peace settlement in the Middle East, even if they did not want to initiate the peace process with the full international conference that the Soviets had been advocating since 1973. Then, there is clear evidence that in 1988 the Soviets actually helped, in the Palestinian-Israeli strand of Middle East peacemaking, to propel a peace process whose first stages clearly promised to be dominated by Washington.[56] These shifts in U.S. and Soviet attitudes toward Arab-Israeli peacemaking promised wide implications for the Soviets' intricate calculations concerning their relationship with Syria.

A larger question to probe is the reasoning behind the Soviets' long opposition to the idea of U.S.-sponsored peace in the Middle East. One part of the reasoning, as frequently expressed in their own media, has historically stemmed from the opportunity such a peace might provide to the United States to expand its regional basing systems. The more political part of Soviet opposition to a *pax Americana* seemed to stem from a desire to be accorded the "equal status" in global affairs to which the Soviets considered their superpower status entitled them. By the end of the 1980s, however, some senior analysts in Moscow were starting to question openly whether the Middle East was still the valuable strategic "prize" that policymakers in Moscow and Washington had long considered it.[57]

Nevertheless, the majority view among Soviet analysts still, until the last months of the decade, retained its stress on the importance of "equal status" in the Arab-

Israeli arena and on the related need to maintain a good relationship with the Syrians. Why? A part of the answer provided by those questioned derived from the region's geographical proximity to the Soviet Union (as contrasted with, for example, southern Africa). Another part of the answer, however, derived from the issue of Soviet "credibility."

In July 1988 veteran Soviet analyst Georgiy Mirskiy was arguing that, at a time when the Soviets were withdrawing at full speed from their previous commitment in Afghanistan, "we cannot abandon Syria, because if we did, people elsewhere, even in Eastern Europe, would see it as a sign of weakness."[58] Clearly, by the end of the decade, this particular line of argument could no longer carry much force with a Soviet leadership that was facing not only the dissolution of the empire in eastern Europe but also serious strains within the Union of Soviet Socialist Republics as well.

In regard to the latter development there arose, at the end of the 1980s, the possibility that a new factor would enter Soviet calculations concerning the Arab-Israeli conflict – a factor that had not had much perceptible force in Soviet decision making since before World War II. This element involved calculating the effect Moscow's policies in the Arab-Israeli situation might have on the prospects of maintaining a workable coalition with the traditionally Muslim populations of Soviet Central Asia. Would this consideration reduce Moscow's willingness to effect a rapprochement with Israel? As of early 1990, there was no evidence available on this question. Should Central Asian considerations eventually significantly affect Moscow's Arab-Israeli policy, however, these essentially domestic considerations might emerge as a major political constraint on the conduct of Soviet policy there. The influence of the other, more global, political factors on Soviet policy-making in the region – the need to demonstrate the credibility of Soviet commitments and the attempt to oppose a *pax Americana* – had, after all, either declined to near zero by the end of the decade or been transformed into something else.

Conclusion: Soviet Policy-Making

The above survey of the Soviet Union's relationship with Syria during the years under study indicates that there was a considerable change in the particular kinds of interests the Soviets were pursuing through the relationship at any one stage. Broadly speaking, the need to prevent a *pax Americana* seemed to propel the relationship in the years 1978 through 1984 or 1985. This need was particularly acute in the early 1980s, when the Soviets perceived the potential for such a peace and the enhanced U.S. strategic ties with a worryingly militarized Israel as twin links in the chain of the Reagan administration's sinister worldwide pursuit of "neoglobalism." Combating the *pax Americana* thus almost inevitably meant that the Soviets would pursue their own enhanced strategic relationship with Syria—even if this involved ceding to Damascus some of the power to drive the pace and structure of the relationship.

After Gorbachev started radically reducing the tension in the relationship with the United States beginning in 1985, the Soviets' motivation in their relationship with Damascus began drawing upon a different mix—one in which building and then maintaining a good political relationship with the United States was paramount. Within this new framework for the relationship with Syria, as John Hannah and others have observed, the Soviets seized back much of the control over the relationship with Syria that they had ceded to Damascus in the years when it had seemed important to win "victories" against the Americans and Israelis in Lebanon.

The implications for the Soviet-Syrian relationship in the following years remained unclear. What did seem clear was that, in the context of an Arab-Israeli peace process that offered real Soviet involvement, Soviet decision makers would likely feel little constrained in their participation by any Syrian reservations—and the Syrian ability to influence the course of Soviet participation would decrease to the degree that the Soviets could strengthen their relations with other potential participants, including Israel.

What if an Arab-Israeli peace process should commence that did not offer serious participation to Moscow? The traditional answer to this since the 1950s had always been that the Soviets would oppose any peace process in the region that offered them less than equal status with the Americans. From the mid-1980s on, however, Soviet analysts were expressing unprecedented concern about the threat to global stability posed by Israel's nuclear and missile capabilities. Meanwhile, there were some hints from Soviet officials that they might be prepared to accept less than equal status with the United States in a peace settlement. In 1988, for example, the CPSU International Department's Karen Brutents described the Middle East as "a very important region for our country, geographically." But he said that the Soviets were prepared to consider U.S. and West European interests in the region, "including your economic interests," and stressed: "We want the level of military activities in the region to be lowered."[59]

If the Soviets should continue to view Israel's nuclear and missile program as a major threat to global stability, then it is possible that in the future they might consider accepting something substantially less than equal peace-making status with the Americans to subdue this threat. Might not some future Soviet policy makers, indeed, consider that the very best way to contain the threat posed by Israel's unconventional weapons programs might be to concur in an Arab-Israeli *pax Americana*? Throughout most of the 1980s, such a conjecture would have seemed farfetched; at the dawn of the 1990s, it appeared to be yet another possible option for Moscow. By the dawn of the 1990s, however, the new imperative for Moscow to deal with the breakdown of the previous contract with Central Asian Muslims might present a new obstacle to such a decision.

5

Beyond Crisis Management?

The preceding analyses of the local Israel-Syria balance, as well as the evolution of the relationships between each of these local powers and its principal superpower backer, offer some explanation of the two specific features of this conflict that were identified in chapter 1 — namely, its relative immunity to the trend toward peaceful resolution of conflicts that was evident in other regions of the Third World in the late 1980s and the stabilization of the situation even in the absence of active diplomacy.

The immunity of the Israeli-Syrian conflict to trends evident elsewhere in the Third World stemmed from two features of its role within the global power balance. The first of these was the disparity, in terms of both power and commitment, between the two superpowers in the broader Arab-Israeli region of which the conflict is a part — a disparity that in both respects favored the United States. The U.S. power superiority was rooted in both the naval superiority that NATO enjoyed in the eastern Mediterranean and the strategic relationships that the United States enjoyed with regional powers including Israel, Egypt (after Camp David), Jordan, and the Gulf states. The Soviets' far smaller naval presence in the Mediterranean, its often difficult relationships with Syria, Libya, and Iraq, and its inferior power projection capabilities could not match the U.S.

ability either to fight its own wars in the region or, more important, to support the war-fighting efforts of its regional partners.

The disparity in the resolve displayed by the two superpowers in the Arab-Israeli region had been demonstrated most memorably in the global alert of nuclear forces that President Nixon had ordered during the 1973 Middle East war. The American resolve thus demonstrated was matched at no period either then or through the end of the 1980s by any indication that Soviet decision makers would be similarly prepared to heighten global tensions in response to Middle Eastern developments.[1]

In 1973 the U.S. superiority over the Soviets in the Arab-Israeli region had been evident in terms of both resolve and power. Five years later, the major effect of the conclusion of the Camp David accords was to bring Egypt unequivocally into military collaboration with the United States. Given the strategic capabilities of Egypt at the regional level, this development even further improved the U.S. position there vis-à-vis the Soviets. The enhanced superiority of the U.S. position that emerged from Camp David then provided the global-level backdrop against which the two superpowers pursued their policies in the region throughout the 1980s.

One major effect of the disparity, in both power and resolve, between the positions of the two superpowers in the Arab-Israeli region was that the United States was able to maintain the veto power it had claimed since 1974 over any attempt at Arab-Israeli peacemaking. Throughout the 1980s, as we have seen, the United States took no action of its own to initiate diplomatic action in the Syrian-Israeli dispute, and it was able to ignore the Soviets' continuing demands for an international conference to resolve all aspects of the Arab-Israeli conflict. Meanwhile, the growing worldwide understanding of U.S. veto power effectively forestalled any sustained attempt by others to bring the dispute to the negotiating table.[2]

The Soviets were, quite simply, unable to mount any

effective challenge to the diplomatic impasse that resulted. To that extent, the relationship between the two superpowers in the Arab-Israeli region no longer, in the 1980s, actually accorded with Alexander George's definition of "disputed interest symmetry," but came closer to resembling his definition of "interest asymmetry favoring the United States."[3] Inasmuch as the Soviets continued to claim an equal role with the United States in Arab-Israeli peacemaking, as the decade progressed this claim came increasingly to resemble a perfunctory, pro forma relic of Brezhnev-era diplomacy. By the end of the decade, moreover, there were some signals that the Soviets might be preparing to retreat from their claim of an equal role in Arab-Israeli peacemaking. This was evident both from the encouragement they gave to PLO Chairman Yasir Arafat during 1987 and 1988 to enter what was clearly going to be—in the initial stages at least—a U.S.-dominated negotiation with Israel and from assurances, such as those given by Karen Brutents in that same period, that the Soviets would be prepared to consider U.S. special interests in the region.

The veto power enjoyed by the United States provided only part of the explanation for the diplomatic stalemate of the Israeli-Syrian conflict in the 1980s. A second part of the explanation must be sought in the anomalous position the conflict occupied in world politics because of two other considerations. Although Israel may be physically located within what is generally regarded as the Third World, it is not a Third World nation; and Israel's relationship with the United States may exhibit some of the features of one between a Third World power and a superpower (primarily, Israel's chronic economic dependency on the United States), but in other important aspects the relationship is markedly different from that between a Third World power and a superpower. Indeed, Israel's influence within the U.S. political system appeared, for at least part of the period covered by the present study, to exceed not only that of any other state located in the Third World, but even that of some of the NATO allies of the United States.[4]

Where Israel and Syria are concerned, this Israeli influence on U.S. policy-making had been embodied since 1974 in the U.S. undertaking to consult with Israel before pursuing any diplomatic initiative. It was also evident throughout the 1980s, however, in the permissiveness with which the United States responded to incidents such as Israel's pursuit of the 1982 invasion beyond the limits originally described for it, the Pollard and Vanunu affairs, and the ballooning cost overruns on the Lavi.

The 1974 undertaking and the relationship it embodied did not, however, give the government of Israel a totally free hand to take any steps it might wish concerning the Syrian issue. That much was clarified when even the very sympathetic Reagan-Haig team in Washington felt obliged to take punitive action to protest the Begin government's extension of Israeli law to the Golan in 1981. But the 1974 undertaking did impede the U.S. pursuit of its own range of options for dealing with this conflict and may well have inhibited U.S. diplomacy at some stages through the end of the 1970s. After President Reagan came into office in 1981, he and his team were generally little inclined to consider any diplomatic resolution of the root causes of the Syrian-Israeli conflict anyway, so the 1974 undertaking cannot be defined as having constrained them from any pursuit of diplomacy. Instead of diplomacy, the prime focus of at least the first Reagan administration, in its rhetoric and its policies, was on seeking to use the military capabilities of Israel (as of other allies in the Third World) to roll back a Soviet Third World empire that they perceived would threaten U.S. interests.

If the first Reagan administration sought to use Israel's military in the same way it was using the mujaheddin in Afghanistan or the contras in Nicaragua, Israel's relationship with Washington was still very different from that enjoyed by those other Reagan Doctrine participants. Thus, when the U.S. political relationship with the Soviet Union started to improve from late 1984 on, it was possible for decision makers in Washington to contemplate scaling back the aid flow to the mujaheddin or the contras, but through the end of the 1980s it would have been political suicide for any U.S. decision maker seriously to have advocated adopting such a policy toward Israel.[5]

The Syrian issue was not the only Middle East issue of concern to both the Israelis and the Americans on which Washington had a long-standing policy of deferring to Israeli preferences. This was also true of the Palestinian issue; however, toward the end of the 1980s, there were some signs that concerning Palestinian matters, Washington was rethinking the policy of always deferring to Israeli wishes. The Reagan administration's December 1988 decision to open the dialogue with the PLO, and the decision of the incoming Bush administration to continue it, were both made despite strong protests from the Israeli government. The independent attitude indicated by those decisions, however, was not, through the end of the decade, replicated by any signs of independent American diplomacy on the Golan question. Nevertheless, the ability of the Reagan and Bush administrations to maintain some independence on the PLO issue had injected a new factor into the U.S.-Israeli relationship that might help to set the stage in the 1990s for successful diplomacy on the Israel-Syria issue.

The other major phenomenon that this study has sought to explain the fact that, even in the absence of any attempts to resolve the dispute between Israel and Syria through diplomatic means, nevertheless major war between them was avoided throughout the 1980s. Such was the outcome, moreover, despite the fact that the two sides engaged in a number of skirmishes in the subsidiary arena of Lebanon, with the broadest of these—the battles of June 1982—occurring during a period of high tension between their superpower backers.

The seemingly anomalous strategic stability displayed in the area even in the absence of peacemaking stemmed from developments at both the regional and the global levels. In keeping with the view that fundamental decisions of war and peace rested primarily with the local parties, the first question to answer is why each of the local powers involved refrained during the period under study from initiating a major war with the other. The special case of June 1982, when Israel's decision to launch a massive invasion of Lebanon would have necessarily involved engaging the Syrian troop deployments there, has been exhaustively addressed in chapter 2. But in that case, too, in keeping with the events of the rest of the decade, the majority view of the Israeli government – if not of General Sharon – was still that the campaign should not escalate to the point where the bulk of Syria's strategic forces might be drawn in.

At the regional level, the fighting of 1982 proved to be a crucial turning point. This was true not primarily because it spurred the Syrian military buildup of the next few years, because (as explained in chapter 2) this buildup never challenged Israel's continuing military superiority; the more significant way in which the events of 1982 and their aftermath affected the regional balance was by forcing the Israelis to start rethinking their national security doctrine.

The casualties that Israel suffered in the 1982–1985 period shocked the nation. Whereas casualties twice as heavy had been considered an acceptable (if high) price to pay to withstand the Syrian-Egyptian offensive of 1973, the casualties of 1982 were deemed unacceptable by a majority in Israel's society and defense community, primarily because the cause for which they had perished remained obscure. This reaction eventually led, following 1982, to the generally accepted conclusion that there were few remaining political objectives that would justify so many casualties in any future large-scale Israeli offensive. And if Israel could meanwhile rely on the continuing and impressive technological advantage it enjoyed in conventional war-fighting capabilities, as well as on its increasingly visible nuclear capabilities, to deter any future attack by its opponents, then it might be possible to ensure the nation's survival without having to fight further major shooting wars at all – offensive or defensive.

Some such train of strategic thinking, as evidenced in many of the Israeli analyses described in chapter 2, seems to have supported the trend toward adopting a doctrine of strategic deterrence that was evident beginning in mid-1988. By the end of the decade, it was still impossible to judge whether this trend had become irreversibly embedded in Israeli doctrine. But it was already clear that Israeli attitudes toward war-fighting had been indelibly affected by the experience in Lebanon. This fact must account for much of the reason why, despite the battlefield superiority Israel continued to enjoy over Syria through the end of the decade, there were no more Israeli "adventures" similar to the one that Sharon had launched in 1982.

If Israel's "Lebanon syndrome" can be said to account for that country's restraint through the end of the 1980s, then the cause of Syria's restraint must be sought elsewhere, because Syria's national security decision makers showed few signs of the war-weariness that was evident in Israel. In Lebanon, the Syrian leadership continued to demonstrate that it was prepared to risk significant casualties among its troops to achieve the political objective of regime survival. Moreover, Syria still had one remaining dispute with Israel—occupation of the Golan—for whose just resolution the leadership continued to declare that it was prepared, under the proper circumstances, to fight.

What had stopped it from doing so through the period under study? According to the admission of the defense minister himself, only the unfavorable strategic balance with Israel. Israel's ability to maintain its strategic superiority, the assistance that it received from the United States in doing so, and the concurrence of the Soviets must, therefore, all be considered contributing factors in deterring the Syrians from initiating war and thus in preventing major war between the two regional powers in the 1980s. (It can be argued that this goal of avoiding a major Syrian-Israeli war could have been achieved at less cost through diplomacy. The possible validity of this argument, however, should not blind us to the fact that a form of strategic stability—however costly or risk-laden—was nonetheless achieved in this situation.)

The second part of the explanation for the strategic

stabilization in the area in the 1980s must consider the actions of the superpowers. As previously mentioned, the latter contributed to the environment in which the local powers made their national security decisions. An analysis of superpower behavior reveals the important conclusion that, by their actions during the period 1982–1985, the two superpowers were both clearly indicating that there should not be another major war in the Syrian-Israeli arena and that they would actively seek to prevent such a war.

The American side demonstrated this most clearly through the firmness with which the Reagan-Haig team delivered the June 9 demarche to the Israeli premier, emphasizing that the United States did not want to see any breakdown of the cease-fire in the eastern Lebanon sector so highly sensitive for Syria. And the Soviet side demonstrated its commitment to avoiding major war in this area most clearly through the limitations it continued to impose on Syria's military capabilities, even while Moscow was helping the Asad regime, in the 1982–1985 period, to engage in the biggest buildup of military power the country had ever seen.

An important question that arises from the above analysis of the superpowers' behavior in 1982–1985 is the degree to which the caution they displayed during those years was a function precisely of the tension that existed between them at the global level. The existence of such tension in the Washington-Moscow relationship might well have increased the wariness with which decision makers in both capitals viewed the prospect of a local war in the Middle East escalating to a global confrontation. The corollary would be that, as the bilateral superpower relationship improved in the latter half of the decade, so, too, might have eroded the willingness of the Soviets and Americans to act to prevent the outbreak of a major Syrian-Israeli war.

On neither the U.S. nor the Soviet side, however, was there any evidence in the late 1980s that this was the case. Indeed, the role of these two powers in the world political order that started emerging in those years promised to be so fundamentally different from the paramountcy they had enjoyed since World War II that many of the "lessons" that might otherwise have been learned from the earlier experience of global détente in the 1970s, concerning the implications of such a détente for Third World stability, might have to be seriously reformulated.

THE IMPROVED SUPERPOWER RELATIONSHIP in the latter 1980s was the primary factor that offered some hope that, in the 1990s, the long-standing conflict between Israel and Syria could be moved from the battlefield to the negotiating table. The new détente between Washington and Moscow allowed the superpowers to emerge from the confines of tightly bipolar partisanship regarding the Israel-Syria confrontation. (Significant, indeed, is the degree to which the Soviet Union was able to improve its relations with Israel in the years following 1985. Although the U.S. relationship with Syria continued to evince both lulls and storms in the latter half of the decade, it was interesting to see how, in the Lebanese elections of 1988, George Shultz's State Department opted to work very closely with Damascus.) Beyond broadening diplomatic options, the new détente allowed the superpowers to consider meaningful joint efforts to reduce tensions in the Arab-Israeli region. Discussions on regional political issues were launched at the assistant secretary level and slowly upgraded.

Beyond the actions that the superpowers themselves could take as international tensions subsided, this development had a broad ripple effect in restructuring the incentives for local partners. In 1982 and 1983, Sharon and Asad had been able to make effective appeals to their superpower partners based on crude references to "the global threat from the other superpower." By the late 1980s, such appeals already seemed outdated; leaders in Israel and Syria had to seek new ways of optimizing their international support.

The causes for optimism that the Israel-Syria confrontation might be defused without recourse to a further war were not limited to developments at the global political level but existed at the local level as well. On the Israeli side, the general recognition that there were limits to the utility of military force (first engendered by the Lebanon experience and then reinforced to some extent by the *intifada*), enabled some Israeli thinkers to move beyond traditional defensive-offensive doctrines and toward consideration of a more sophisticated doctrine of deterrence and of an eventual normalization of Israel's situation in the region. For such shifts to take place in any lasting way, a stable peace would be necessary with all of Israel's neighbors, including Syria. Meanwhile, Israel's satellite as well as other reconnaissance capabilities could eventually enable its leaders to conceive of a secure and stable peace involving replacing the IDF's ground presence in Golan with a return of effective Syrian sovereignty, under an internationally guaranteed demilitarization regime, which the Israelis themselves could also monitor from afar, as part of an overall peace agreement.

On the Syrian side, the fears persisted that Syria would be unable to negotiate effectively with Israel from a position of military inferiority. By the late 1980s, however, two key components of the international environment in which the Syrian leadership operated were pushing it toward accepting serious negotiations with Israel – the Soviet position and general political trends within the Arab world. Pressures from major players within each of these parts of Syria's environment, coupled with reassurances that Syria would not be excluded from any future Arab-Israeli negotiations, could potentially bring the Syrian regime to the table. The rapprochement between Syria and Egypt that appeared initially at the end of the 1980s held the promise that Syria might be drawing closer to the kinds of nonmilitary strategies that the Egyptians had pursued to resolve their part of the conflict with Israel.[6]

The above developments all provided some cause for hope that a serious U.S. commitment to working for a negotiated resolution of the Israeli-Syrian conflict might effect some worthwhile results. Yet, such Arab-Israeli diplomacy as the United States was cautiously attempting toward the end of the 1980s still limited its purview to dealing with the Israeli-Palestinian parts of the conflict because American officials judged that bringing Syria into the diplomacy would cause potentially crippling complications.

In none of its Middle East diplomacy in the 16 years after 1974 did the United States demonstrate a serious commitment to resolving the Golan issue—a necessary first step to bring the Israeli-Syrian dispute back to the negotiating table. Yet, the Israel-Syria arena hosted ever more fearsome arsenals which, if the conflict between the two states should remain unresolved, could catapult the entire region into a far deadlier war than any it had ever seen.

Within the United States, changes in public attitudes in the latter 1980s were already affecting the way the political system reacted to issues of concern in the Middle East. The Reagan and Bush administrations won broad public support for their decisions to open and then continue the dialogue with the PLO. A decision to reopen serious talks over the long-term status of the Golan might not win such rapid political support. But within the context of a general transformation of the Middle East from a military tinderbox into an area of productive human enterprise, such a step might prove surprisingly popular. It would also be an essential guarantee for the long-term viability of all other peace agreements between Israel and its neighbors—including any future settlement with the Palestinians as well as the Camp David treaty with Egypt.

Notes

Chapter 1

1. It should be noted, however, that one other deep-seated "regional" conflict, that between India and Pakistan, also failed to respond to the superpower détente of the late 1980s by moving toward a negotiated resolution. Indeed, the conflict between the two large South Asian states seemed to grow hotter as the 1980s came to an end.

2. This was not the case for the partly derivative, partly autonomous offshoot of the Israeli-Syrian conflict in Lebanon, which, at the end of the 1980s, seemed once again to be spinning out of control. In that period, however, unlike earlier in the 1980s, instability in Lebanon did not threaten to draw Israel and Syria into a direct confrontation.

3. The entire text of Saddam Hussein's speech, and the way it was reported by his national news agency, can be found in Foreign Broadcast Information Service—Near East and South Asia (hereafter FBIS-NES) 90-064, April 3, 1990, pp. 32–36.

4. The experience of acute, nuclear-level crises such as the Cuban missile crisis or the Arab-Israeli war of October 1973 necessarily leaves an unpleasant aftereffect in the relationship between the superpowers. In 1962 this unpleasantness was tempered in both Washington and Moscow by a new realization of the enormity of the decisions the leaders had confronted and by a determination both to abide by the resolution reached for the

immediate crisis in Cuba and to institute a more effective crisis-management regime (the "Hotline" agreement). In the aftermath of the 1973 crisis, by contrast, the mood in both superpower homelands remained one of hurt and distrust. And instead of viewing peacemaking in the Arab-Israeli conflict as a useful forum for joint U.S.-Soviet activity, the United States tried to use the postcrisis period to achieve a political advantage against the Soviets in the region.

5. For a review of some of this evidence, see Helena Cobban, "Israel's Nuclear Game: The U.S. Stake," *World Policy Journal* 5, no. 3 (Summer 1988): 424–425.

6. The Israeli scholar Shai Feldman has written that "America's commitment to Israel's survival, security, and welfare never constituted an interest 'per se,'" but that it evolved instead "from an ideological and cultural affinity toward the Jewish state." Shai Feldman, *U.S. Middle East Policy: The Domestic Setting* (Jerusalem: Jerusalem Post, and Boulder, Colo.: Westview, 1988), 2. My view, however, is that even if the U.S. commitment to Israel is not a direct interest but a derived interest, it will nevertheless for the foreseeable future have all the force of a direct interest in most conceivable scenarios short of global nuclear war. See chapter 3.

7. Alexander L. George, ed., *Managing U.S.-Soviet Rivalry: Problems of Crisis Prevention* (Boulder, Colo.: Westview, 1983), 385.

8. One contrast here would be with the Iran-Iraq theater, one in which both superpowers have a high level of interests, but where the bitter fighting of 1980–1988 failed to spark a crisis between the superpowers.

9. Alexander L. George, "U.S.-Soviet Efforts to Cooperate in Crisis Management and Crisis Avoidance," *U.S.-Soviet Security Cooperation: Achievements, Failures, Lessons*, Alexander L. George, Philip J. Farley, and Alexander Dallin, eds. (New York and Oxford: Oxford University Press, 1988), 583–585.

For many years, influential Soviet intellectuals tried to engage their Western counterparts in formalizing some "code of conduct" for superpower behavior in the Third World. U.S. diplomacy has traditionally been wary of such efforts, however, and Soviet President Mikhail S. Gorbachev and Foreign Minister Eduard A. Shevardnadze have placed their primary emphasis on strengthening the role of the United Nations Security Council in resolving regional conflicts.

10. George, "U.S.-Soviet Efforts," 584.

11. Author interview with Col.-Gen. Dmitri Volkogonov, Moscow, July 1988.

12. Ibid. Volkogonov also said that in 1982 neither super-power had planned to introduce its own forces into the conflict.

13. George, "U.S.-Soviet Efforts," 584.

14. *The Military Balance, 1989–1990* (London: IISS, 1989), 115.

15. Raymond L. Garthoff, *Détente and Confrontation* (Washington, D.C.: Brookings Institution, 1985), 591.

16. For a concise account of developments throughout this watershed, see Gordon R. Weihmiller and Dusko Doder, *U.S.-Soviet Summits: An Account of East-West Diplomacy at the Top, 1955–1985* (Washington, D.C.: Institute for the Study of Diplomacy, and Lanham, Md.: University Press of America, 1986), 109–119.

17. This is also the conclusion reached by John P. Hannah. See his monograph, *At Arms Length: Soviet-Syrian Relations in the Gorbachev Era* (Washington, D.C.: Washington Institute for Near East Policy, 1989), 56.

Chapter 2

1. Despite the emphasis of both sides on the primacy of this confrontation, at times each behaved as though it were subordinate to other concerns — Israel, when it struck deep into Lebanon in 1982, and Syria when it reacted to Iraqi-generated or other internal or external security challenges. Nevertheless, the major military establishments of both parties continued to act throughout this period as though they considered this front to be the principal one in their strategic planning.

2. Patrick Seale, *Asad of Syria: The Struggle for the Middle East* (London: I. B. Tauris, 1988), 495.

3. The text of this previously secret document was released in Michael Widlanski, ed., *Can Israel Survive a Palestinian State?* (Jerusalem: Institute for Advanced Strategic and Political Studies, 1990), 120–121. Ze'ev Schiff had referred to the second of these undertakings in his article, "Dealing with Syria," *Foreign Policy*, no. 55 (Summer 1984), 96–97.

4. For example, Ze'ev Schiff's judgment in a 1989 study that

"nuclear weapons have never been intended by Israel for use in anything other than a worst-case scenario" addressed this topic with unprecedented frankness. Ze'ev Schiff, *Security for Peace: Israel's Minimal Security Requirements in Negotiations with the Palestinians* (Washington, D.C.: Washington Institute for Near East Policy, 1989), 28.

5. *The Military Balance, 1978–1979* (London: International Institute for Strategic Studies, 1979), compared with the 1987–1988 edition.

6. See, for example, "Navy Reportedly Confronts Two Israeli Ships," *Al-Ra'y al-'amm* (Kuwait), March 21, 1989, p. 24, as translated in FBIS-NES-89-155, March 23, 1989, p. 44.

7. See, for example, Kenneth Kaplan, "Syrian Naval Action off Coast of Lebanon Not Seen as Aimed at Israel," *Jerusalem Post*, July 12, 1989, p. 12.

8. Schiff, "Dealing with Syria," 92. See also Helena Cobban, "Thinking about Lebanon," *American-Arab Affairs*, no. 12 (Spring 1985).

9. Yair Evron, *War and Intervention in Lebanon: The Israeli-Syrian Deterrence Dialogue* (Baltimore: Johns Hopkins University Press, 1987), 79. Chapter 6 of Evron's book gives a sophisticated account of the Israeli-Syrian deterrence equation in Lebanon. Evron occasionally refers to linkages between the Lebanon and Golan fronts, but he does not locate his discussion of the two countries' interactions in Lebanon within the broad context of their overall combat capabilities, including their "strategic"-level capabilities.

10. Communication from Ze'ev Schiff, October 1989. Yair Evron wrote that, as they were defined in a March 1976 Israeli communication to Washington, the Red Lines were much more restrictive on the Syrians (Evron, *War and Intervention*, 46–47). Possibly, however, the items Evron listed constituted an earlier Israeli wish list.

11. See Evron, *War and Intervention*, 52–56.

12. For the texts of the Camp David accords and the treaty, see William B. Quandt, *Camp David: Peacemaking and Politics* (Washington, D.C.: Brookings Institution, 1986), Appendixes G and I.

13. For a review of these developments, see ibid., 32–33.

14. See Ze'ev Schiff, *A History of the Israeli Army, 1874 to the Present* (New York: Macmillan, 1985), 55–56. Schiff writes that

after Israel's 1967 victory, there was a renewed debate over troop reductions, but that these led nowhere because of the speedy resumption of border fighting in the War of Attrition (p. 178).

15. Author interview with Zvi Lanir, Jerusalem, July 1987.

16. See Anthony H. Cordesman, *The Arab-Israeli Military Balance and the Art of Operations* (Washington, D.C.: American Enterprise Institute for Public Policy Research, 1987), 47–51; and Schiff, *A History of the Israeli Army*, 228–229.

17. Forces from a number of other Arab countries had joined the Syrian and Egyptian war effort in 1973. But their numbers were extremely limited, they arrived at the front only in the latter days of the fighting, and their ability to work effectively with their host forces was minimal. In the absence of any serious inter-Arab military planning or joint exercises, these would be the most likely features of any future combination of forces.

18. For a good description of Israeli decision making concerning the Litani Operation, see Evron, *War and Intervention*, 74–82.

19. Author interview with Dan Horowitz, Jerusalem, 1987.

20. Ze'ev Schiff and Ehud Ya'ari, *Israel's Lebanon War* (New York: Simon and Schuster, 1984), 31.

21. Seale, *Asad of Syria*, 313.

22. The trend lines over time in the defense expenditures of each country, as shown in figure 1, are significant. But direct comparisons between these dollar figures can be misleading, owing to the different pricing formulas used for Eastern bloc arms and other factors. For the sake of the present study, the more interesting comparisons are those between the percentage of GDP devoted by each country to defense (figure 2), and the defense manpower burdens on each country (table 1).

23. Seale, *Asad of Syria*, 347. Seale also noted that, for Asad, "parity was not just a matter of striking a military balance with Israel but of matching it right across the board, in education, technology, social progress and external alliances, as well as in purely armed strength." (Ibid.)

24. Author interview with Syrian Foreign Minister Farouq al-Sharaa, Damascus, July 1987.

25. In 1948 the Soviet Union was the first great power to recognize the newly established state of Israel.

26. For details of this period, see Efraim Karsh, *The Soviet Union and Syria: The Asad Years* (London: Royal Institute of International Affairs, and New York: Routledge, Chapman & Hall, 1988), 48–53.

27. For details of this affair, see ibid., 55–56, and Kassem M. Ja'far, "The Soviet Union in the Middle East: A Case Study of Syria," *Soviet Interests in the Third World*, Robert Cassen, ed. (London: Royal Institute of International Affairs, and Beverly Hills: SAGE, 1985), 269.

28. For a full description of this episode, see Schiff and Ya'ari, *Israel's Lebanon War*, 31–35. Professor Dan Horowitz, in a July 1987 interview, echoed the judgment that it had been Israel that broke the Red Lines agreements.

29. For details, see Helena Cobban, *The Palestinian Liberation Organization: People, Power and Politics* (New York: Cambridge University Press, 1984), 111.

30. For Schiff and Ya'ari's assessment of the effects of the cabinet changes, see their *Israel: Lebanon War*, 38–40.

31. Schiff, "Dealing with Syria," 102.

32. Evron, *War and Intervention*, 132.

33. Schiff and Ya'ari, *Israel's Lebanon War*, 41–44. Yair Evron disagreed with these writers over the extent of the Israeli decision makers' war aims vis-à-vis the Syrians. He wrote: "It was argued that Syrian military power should be destroyed before it could be used against Israel. Shattering the Syrian forces would postpone Syria's war plans indefinitely. Alternatively, a war would reinforce the effect of Israel's deterrence against any Syrian-initiated war in the future." Evron, *War and Intervention*, 116. There is no evidence, however, that the Israelis planned to strike Syrian forces in Syria, which is where Asad kept most of them during the 1982 battles (see below).

34. Evron, *War and Intervention*, 125.

35. Author interview with Ariel Sharon, Jerusalem, July 1987.

36. Evron, *War and Intervention*, 128.

37. Schiff and Ya'ari, *Israel's Lebanon War*, 157–162.

38. Evron, *War and Intervention*, 136.

39. Seale, *Asad of Syria*, 382.

40. Evron, *War and Intervention*, 131, 137. For details of the air battles, see Seale, *Asad of Syria*, 381–382; and Helena Cobban, "The Air-Defense Lessons of the Lebanese War of June 1982: The Soviet View," *Soviet Armed Forces Review Annual, Volume 10* (1985–1986), David R. Jones, ed. (Gulf Breeze, Fla.: Academic International Press, 1987).

41. Schiff and Ya'ari, *Israel's Lebanon War*, 159.

42. Arye Naor, *Cabinet at War* (published in Hebrew, in Is-

rael, 1987), 76. An English translation of this is provided in William B. Quandt, *The Arab-Israeli Conflict: Implications for Mediterranean Security*, Adelphi Papers, no. 230 (London: IISS, 1988), 6–7.

43. Evron, *War and Intervention*, 137.

44. Seale, *Asad of Syria*, 383.

45. Author background interviews with U.S. participants, 1987 and 1988.

46. Evron, *War and Intervention*, 137.

47. Author interview with Ariel Sharon, Jerusalem, July 1987.

48. Evron, *War and Intervention*, 142.

49. See Cobban, *The Palestinian Liberation Organization*, 121–126.

50. Seale, *Asad of Syria*, 390.

51. Arafat made a point of traveling not through Syria, but on a boat that – in a further snub to Asad – made a port call in Egypt. The PLO chairman managed to leave Beirut with the PLO's standing in Arab and world public opinion enhanced by its performance under the Israeli onslaught – and with more than a hint that, in the new round of Arab-Israeli diplomacy, Palestinian aspirations would receive some consideration. For Asad, who had (probably wisely, from his point of view) decided to sit out as much as he could of the Lebanese fighting, Arafat's aura of glory only rubbed further salt into the wound of his country's humiliation.

52. Cobban, *The Palestinian Liberation Organization*, 128–130.

53. For the text of these assurances, see "Plan for the Departure of the PLO from Beirut," in U.S. Department of State, *American Foreign Policy Current Documents, 1982* (Washington, D.C., 1985), 837–839.

54. Seale, *Asad of Syria*, 395.

55. See Helena Cobban, *The Making of Modern Lebanon* (Boulder, Colo.: Westview, 1985), 187–208.

56. This point was also recognized by Yair Evron in *War and Intervention* (202–206), though he does not codify the nature of the two sides' interests.

57. Barukh Ron, "3290 Widows, 4669 Orphans," *Bamahane* (Tel Aviv), no. 30 (April 1986): 7; as translated in Joint Publications Research Service–Near East and South Asia (hereafter JPRS-NEA) 86-093, p. 29. Other Israeli sources generally refer

to 600 or 650 dead. Arab losses in the months June–August 1982 were estimated at over 19,000 dead (see "Chronology," *Middle East Journal* 37, no. 2 [Spring 1983]: 250).

58. The Department of Defense's own fact-finding commission would later conclude that "the presence mission was not interpreted the same by all levels of the chain of command." See *Report of the DOD Commission on Beirut International Airport Terrorist Attack, October 23, 1983* (Washington, D.C.: GPO, December 20, 1983), 134.

59. See Cobban, *The Making of Modern Lebanon*, 90–92.

60. For details of the political struggles that accompanied Asad's illness, see Seale, *Asad of Syria*, 421–440.

61. Ibid., 424. Seale also wrote that Asad told his top generals that "the advancement of Rif'at was an American-Saudi plot to unseat him." Ibid.

62. Geoffrey Kemp, "Lessons of Lebanon: A Guideline for Future U.S. policy," *Middle East Insight* 6, nos. 1–2 (Summer 1988): 65. See also, Cobban, *The Making of Modern Lebanon*, 202–205, and William B. Quandt, "Reagan's Lebanon Policy: Trial and Error," in *Middle East Journal* 38, no. 2 (Spring 1984).

63. Kemp, "Lessons of Lebanon," 65.

64. Seale, *Asad of Syria*, 417.

65. Figures from *The Military Balance, 1987–1988*, p. 114, and *1989–1990*, p. 115.

66. Seale, *Asad of Syria*, 398.

67. Ibid., 397. The Soviets were able to learn many useful lessons about NATO's counter-air-defense capabilities from these visits. For details, see Cobban, "The Air-Defense Lessons," 266–268.

68. Author interview with Mustafa Tlas, Damascus, July 1987. See also Seale, *Asad of Syria*, 398.

69. See Cobban, "The Air-Defense Lessons," 260.

70. Aharon Levran and Zeev Eytan, eds., *The Middle East Military Balance 1986* (Jerusalem: Jerusalem Post, and Boulder, Colo.: Westview, 1987), 187 (hereafter *MEMB-86*).

71. Editions of *The Military Balance* for the years between 1982 and 1987.

72. Ibid.

73. Author interview with a Pentagon official who requested anonymity, November 1989.

74. Author background interview with a Western military expert, July 1987.

75. The oil price collapse meant much lower Baghdad Summit contributions from the Gulf states and lower remittances from the Syrian expatriate workers in the Gulf.

76. *MEMB-86*, p. 178.

77. Seale, *Asad of Syria*, 399.

78. Between 1984 and 1985, the Soviets did apparently hand over control of the SAM-5 sites to the Syrians. It is possible that they retained some control over key components of the SAM-5 fire-control systems or of the associated radars, however, and although the nature of the control over the SS-21s is not known, the best estimate is that the Soviets would have insisted at least on some kind of dual-key system for them.

79. Author interview with Mohamed Heikal, Cairo, June 1987.

80. TASS report, "In a Friendly Atmosphere," *Pravda*, April 25, 1987, p. 2, as translated in Foreign Broadcast Information Service–Soviet Union (hereafter FBIS-SOV), April 28, 1987, pp. H7–H8.

81. See Schiff and Ya'ari, *Israel's Lebanon War*, 215–216.

82. Ibid., 283–284.

83. Ibid. Sharon remained in the cabinet even after Begin himself withdrew from public life in September 1983.

84. "Ariel Sharon Assesses Lebanon War," *Yedi'ot Aharonot*, May 24, 1985, weekend supplement, 7, and May 31, 1985, weekend supplement, 2, 7, as translated in JPRS-NEA-85-124, p. 79.

85. Yehoshua Saguy, "IDF Commanders Discuss War Goals, Accomplishments," *Yedi'ot Aharonot*, September 17 and 26, 1982, as translated in JPRS 82434, p. 95. Soviet arms transfers to Syria over the next few months made Saguy's conclusions even more valid.

86. Martin Van Creveld, "Not Exactly a Triumph," *Jerusalem Post*, December 10, 1982, weekend supplement, 6, 7, as reproduced in JPRS 82577, pp. 48–49. See also "Rabin Instructs IDF High Command to Discuss Wald Report," *Hadashot*, May 19, 1986, p. 5, as translated in JPRS, NEA-86-083, p. 28.

87. Zvi Lanir, "Political Aims and Military Objectives – Some Observations on the Israeli Experience," *Israeli Security Planning in the 1980s: Its Politics and Economics*, Zvi Lanir, ed. (New York: Praeger, and Tel Aviv: Jaffee Center, 1984), 42.

88. Author interview with Zvi Lanir, July 1987.

89. See, for example, Zvi Timor, "Defense Budget: Strategy

Error since 1967," *'Al Hamishmar*, March 26, 1985, p. 9, as translated in JPRS-NEA-85-073, pp. 73–74; and Alex Fishman, "The
IDF: The Lessons of Lebanon," *'Al Hamishmar*, June 5, 1985,
pp. 6–11, as translated in JPRS-NEA-85-134, p. 46.

90. See, for example, Fishman, "The IDF," and Eliezer Sheffer, "The Economic Burden of the Arms Race between the Confrontation States and Israel," in Lanir, *Israeli Security Planning
in the 1980s*, 42.

91. Ronald Reagan's statement at the departure of Yitzhak
Shamir, November 29, 1983, as reproduced in Toby Dershowitz,
eds., *The Reagan Administration and Israel, Key Statements*
(Washington, D.C.: AIPAC, 1987), 20. The Americans have always stressed the anti-Soviet aspect of the collaboration to allay
any apprehension among U.S. allies in the Arab world who fear
that it might be used against them.

92. "Cost of Lebanon War to Date," *Jerusalem Post*, March
22, 1985, p. 1, as reproduced in JPRS-NEA-85-069, p. 101.

93. Inflation figures from successive editions of *The Military Balance*, using the latest figures available.

94. *MEMB-86*, p. 135. From 1985 on, all U.S. military assistance to Israel was given on a grant basis.

95. Ibid., 135–138.

96. For a codification of the operational lessons that the Israelis learned in Lebanon, including the need to upgrade their
urban and mountain warfare capabilities, see Cordesman, *The
Arab-Israeli Military Balance*, 97–105.

97. *MEMB-86*, pp. 137–138.

98. For information on the Lavi affair, see Joshua Brilliant,
"The Lavi Project: Plane That Shouldn't Have Been," *Jerusalem
Post*, July 1, 1987, p. 6; "General David 'Ivri interviewed on Lavi
project," *Bita'on Heyl Ha'avir* (Tel Aviv), nos. 50–51 (April 1986):
16–20, as translated in JPRS-NEA-86-083, p. 33; and Dov Zakheim, "Yet the Lavi Lingers On and On . . . ," *Washington Times*,
August 26, 1987, p. D2.

99. See David Makovsky, "Rabin to Get U.S. 'Sweetener'
to Scrap Lavi," *Jerusalem Post*, July 1, 1987, p. 1; Judy Maltz,
"General Dynamics Will Buy $800m Worth of Goods Here," *Jeru-
salem Post International Edition* (hereafter *JPIE*), February 27,
1988, p. 6.

100. See "Saar-5s Approved," *Defense and Foreign Affairs
Weekly*, April 4–10, 1988, p. 2. Information on the size of the eventual deal from Ze'ev Schiff, communication of November 1989.

101. See *MEMB-86*, pp. 138–141.

102. "Interview with Manpower Branch Chief," *Bamahane* (Tel Aviv), November 20, 1985, pp. 9–10, as translated in JPRS-NEA-86-008, p. 54.

103. Ze'ev Schiff, "Z. Schiff Series on IDF's Image and Values," *Ha'aretz*, August 2, 4, 5, 7, and 8, 1985, as translated by the Israeli Government Press Office and reproduced in JPRS-NEA-85-129, pp. 45–51.

104. Reuven Pedahtzur, "Operational Norms in the IDF: What's Happening?" *Ha'aretz*, March 4, 1986, as translated in JPRS-NEA-86-046, p. 59.

105. See *New York Times*, November 26, 1987, p. 1.

106. For an interesting exploration of some of the issues raised in this regard, see Danny Rubinstein, "The Best Arm-Breakers May Be the Next Commanders," *Davar*, August 4, 1989, as translated in *Israel Press Briefs*, no. 67 (September 1989): 17–18.

107. For some reporting on these issues, see, for example, items from FBIS-NES-88-026, pp. 40–41.

108. Asher Wallfish, "Shomron: IDF 'Cannot Change Palestinian Will,'" *Jerusalem Post*, August 17, 1988, p. 2, as reproduced in FBIS-NES-88-161, p. 21.

109. A. Wallfish, J. Greenberg, and J. Brilliant, "Uprising Costs IDF NIS 270 Million since Dec.," *Jerusalem Post*, July 11, 1988, as reproduced in FBIS-NES-88-134, p. 28.

110. "Too Many Eggs in the Military Basket," *JPIE*, December 5, 1987, p. 20.

111. Ya'acov Friedler, "Wanted: Statecraft, Not More Arms," *JPIE*, January 2, 1988, p. 9.

112. "Clear Opposition in the IDF to Amos Satellite," *Jerusalem Post*, October 5, 1988, pp. 1, 12; as reproduced in FBIS-NES-88-193, p. 28.

113. "An Achievement That Calls for Decisions," *'Al Hamishmar*, September 20, 1988, p. 1, as translated in FBIS-NES-88-183, p. 18. Ze'ev Schiff warned in a thoughtful analysis that "the United States can say that such a move on the part of Israel is liable to accelerate the arms race in the Middle East.... The Americans will probably demand to know why the launch had to take place now, when Washington is at the height of its efforts to restrict and locate the sale of Chinese missiles to Syria and other Arab countries." See Ze'ev Schiff, "The Reactions That Will Follow the Launch," *Ha'aretz*, September 20, 1988, p. 13, as translated in FBIS-NES-88-183, p. 19.

114. "Rabin Warns Arabs against Use of Chemical Weapons," on Jerusalem radio, July 20, 1988, as translated in FBIS-NES-88-140, p. 29.

115. "Rabin Interviewed on Syrian Threat, Uprising," *Jerusalem Post*, September 11, 1988, p. 4, as reproduced in FBIS-NES-88-176, pp. 37–38.

116. "Rabin Warns Arabs," 29.

117. "Shomron Comments on 'Preemptive' Attack on Syria," *Davar*, September 11, 1988, p. 18, as translated in FBIS-NES-88-176, p. 39. Shomron also said that even if Israel should prove able to develop an ATBM system capable of countering some proportion of the Syrian SSMs, he did not think that such a system could "hermetically seal the entire State of Israel." (Ibid., p. 40.)

118. Hirsh Goodman and W. Seth Carus, *The Future Battlefield and the Arab-Israeli Conflict* (New Brunswick, N.J., and London: Transaction Publishers, 1990), 49–50.

119. Ze'ev Schiff, "Do the Syrians Want War?" *Ha'aretz*, March 14, 17, 18, and 19, 1986, as translated in JPRS-NEA-86-048, p. 44.

120. "Rabin Interviewed on Defense, Political Issues," on Jerusalem TV, December 22, 1985, as translated in FBIS-NES, December 23, 1985, p. I2; and "Rabin Interviewed on Syrian Threat, Uprising," 37–38.

121. "Tlas Interviewed on Iran, Israel, Lebanon," *Al-Anba'* (Kuwait), August 15, 1989, p. 23, as translated in FBIS-NES-89-158, August 17, 1989, p. 31. For some insight into Tlas's relationship with Asad, see "Defense Minister Discusses Asad, Various Issues," *Al-Mustaqbal* (Paris), February 27, 1988, pp. 46–48 (as translated in JPRS-NEA-88-026, pp. 28–32), in which Tlas describes his 35-year friendship with Asad, terming the latter "the Hegel of our time."

122. Syrian Defense Minister Mustafa Tlas claimed in a 1987 interview with the author that former Soviet Premier Aleksei Kosygin had promised that, if the Israelis used nuclear weapons against "Soviet friends," the Soviets would respond in kind. In a 1989 press interview, Tlas said that if Syria were hit by Israel's atomic bombs, "the USSR would give us atomic bombs to attack Israel" ("Tlas Interviewed on Iran, Israel, Lebanon," 32). The latter of these scenarios would not appear to be sufficiently feasible under operational conditions to offer a realistic counter-deterrent to the Israelis. And, in the absence of any of the corrob-

oration from the Soviet side that would be necessary to constitute an ironclad guarantee, Tlas's claims seemed more likely to
constitute a part of the rhetorical bombast for which he was
famed than any credible Syrian counter in kind to Israel's nuclear
deterrent.

123. For discussion of this question, see some of the contributions to Louis Rene Beres, *Security or Armageddon: Israel's
Nuclear Strategy* (Lexington, Mass.: Lexington Books, 1986).

124. For details of this affair, see Evron, *War and Intervention*, 172–174.

125. For Patrick Seale's account of the affair, see Seale,
Asad of Syria, 475–482.

126. We do not know how Asad would have treated Khuly if
the incident had indeed threatened to precipitate a serious Israeli
punishment. And one has to consider the counterrisks involved
for his core interest of political survival if he had moved abruptly
against Khuly, who was described by Patrick Seale as one of
Asad's three "most trusted associates" in security and intelligence matters. (See ibid., 428.)

127. Author interview, Damascus, July 1987. Syria's decision, in December 1989, to restore the diplomatic relations with
Egypt that had been broken at the time of Sadat's peace initiative 12 years before may have signaled the beginning of a Syrian
reassessment on this score.

128. "Shomron Comments," 40.

Chapter 3

1. Steven L. Spiegel, *The Other Arab-Israeli Conflict: Making America's Middle East Policy, from Truman to Reagan* (Chicago: Chicago University Press, 1985), 159–160.

2. Yoram Peri has also noted that the initial entry of military professionals into first-rank positions in the Israeli cabinet, a process that would intensify over the years that followed,
occurred in this same period. (In 1974, Rabin himself would become prime minister.) See Yoram Peri, *Between Battles and Bal-
lots: Israeli Military in Politics* (New York: Cambridge University Press, 1983), 103–104.

3. See Spiegel, *The Other Arab-Israeli Conflict*, 159–164,
and William B. Quandt, *Decade of Decisions: American Policy*

toward the Arab-Israeli Conflict, 1967–76 (Berkeley, Calif.: University of California Press, 1977), 65–68.

4. See, for example, William Safire, *Before the Fall: An Inside View of the Pre-Watergate White House* (Garden City, N.Y.: Doubleday, 1975), 567; and Spiegel, *The Other Arab-Israeli Conflict*, 179.

5. Bernard Reich, *The United States and Israel: Influence in the Special Relationship* (New York: Praeger, 1984), 148–149.

6. Interview with Andrew W. Marshall, February 1988. For an appraisal of Kissinger's relative weight in Ford's decision making, see Spiegel, *The Other Arab-Israeli Conflict*, 286 and 312–314.

7. See, for example, Jimmy Carter, *Keeping Faith: Memoirs of a President* (New York: Bantam, 1982), 274.

8. See Reich, *The United States and Israel*, 148–149.

9. Ronald Reagan, "Recognizing the Israeli Asset," *Washington Post*, August 15, 1979, p. 25.

10. Quoted in *Near East Report*, January 9, 1980, p. 7.

11. Jeane J. Kirkpatrick, *The Reagan Phenomenon and Other Speeches on Foreign Policy* (Washington, D.C.: American Enterprise Institute, 1983), 118.

12. Wolf Blitzer, *Between Washington and Jerusalem: A Reporter's Notebook* (New York and Oxford: Oxford University Press, 1985), 61.

13. Weinberger came to the Pentagon from the San Francisco-based engineering firm Bechtel Inc., which had numerous contracts in the Arab world. But that may not have been a decisive or immutable factor influencing Weinberger's thinking on Middle East issues, as was indicated later in the Reagan years when fellow Bechtel alumnus George P. Shultz became one of Israel's strongest supporters ever as secretary of state.

14. For details, see Laurence I. Barrett, *Gambling with History: Ronald Reagan in the White House* (New York: Penguin, 1984), 273.

15. For this evaluation, see ibid., 276, and Reich, *The United States and Israel*, 105.

16. Author interview with former U.S. official who requested anonymity, March 1988.

17. Samuel Lewis, "An American Perspective on Strategic Cooperation," *Strategy and Defense in the Eastern Mediterranean: An American-Israeli Dialogue*, Robert Satloff, ed. (Wash-

ington, D.C.: Washington Institute for Near East Policy, 1987), 100.

18. Menachem Meron, "An Israeli Perspective on Strategic Cooperation," in Satloff, ed., *Strategy and Defense*, 107. In October 1981, Meron himself was reported as preferring, "at this point, not to expand the strategic cooperation between the two countries." See Yosef Pri'el, "Relations with American Military Establishment," *Davar*, October 19, 1981, p. 12, as translated in JPRS 79813 (January 1982), 72.

19. The text of the agreement appeared in *New York Times*, December 1, 1981, p. A14.

20. Eric Rozenman, *United States–Israel Strategic Cooperation: Conversations and Comments* (Washington, D.C.: Jewish Institute for National Security Affairs, 1989), 8. See also Ambassador Samuel W. Lewis's description of this dilemma in ibid., 13–14.

21. See Foreign Broadcast Information Service–Middle East (hereafter FBIS-ME), December 1, 1981, p. I2. Samuel Lewis has written that, in the negotiations, Sharon described the scope of future strategic cooperation in grandiose, far-reaching terms. "He suggested potential roles that Israel might play in a mutually beneficial alliance that sent cold shivers down the backs of most of the people on the American side of the table." Lewis, "An American Perspective on Strategic Cooperation," 100.

22. Barrett, *Gambling with History*, 277.

23. See Schiff and Ya'ari, *Israel's Lebanon War*, 72–75.

24. Ze'ev Schiff, "Green Light, Lebanon," *Foreign Policy*, no. 50 (Spring 1983): 75.

25. See Alexander M. Haig, Jr., *Caveat: Realism, Reagan, and Foreign Policy* (New York: Macmillan, 1984), 327. In implicit corroboration of Schiff's contention that "Haig issued no threat against Israel's forthcoming military action," Haig made no mention here of any threats having been delivered.

26. Author interview with Zvi Lanir, Jerusalem, July 1987.

27. Steven R. Weisman wrote that "according to Mr. Haig's friends, the immediate cause of his offer to resign was a concern that he was being undercut by Mr. Clark in the Middle East. White House aides acknowledged that Mr. Clark favored a tougher policy toward Israel." "Secretary's Split with President Long in Making," *New York Times*, June 27, 1982, pp. 1, 18.

28. Two such analyses had titles of telling condescension. They were Nimrod Novik, *Encounter with Reality: Reagan and*

the Middle East (The First Term) (Tel Aviv: Jaffee Center, and Boulder, Colo.: Westview, 1985), and Martin Indyk, "Reagan and the Middle East: Learning the Art of the Possible," *SAIS Review* 7, no. 1 (Winter-Spring 1987): 111–138.

29. Indyk, "Reagan and The Middle East," 123. Samuel W. Lewis, who was U.S. ambassador to Israel at the time, has corroborated this assessment. See Lewis, "An American Perspective on Strategic Cooperation," 103.

30. This was also the view of Bernard Gwertzman. See his article, "Reagan Turns to Israel," *New York Times Magazine*, November 27, 1983, p. 65.

31. Ibid., 63. On at least two previous occasions, the Israelis had already been the beneficiaries of a similar waiver of normal FMS provisions. In 1977 it had received permission to use $107 million of FMS funds to produce its locally designed Merkava tank. In September 1981, in an effort to mute Israeli opposition to the Saudi AWACS sale (which would net $8.5 billion for the U.S. economy), Haig had offered the Israelis $200 million in FMS sales "to be applied largely to purchases from their own defense industry." See the uncensored draft of the June 1983 U.S. General Accounting Office report, "U.S. assistance to the State of Israel" (as circulated by the Arab-American Antidiscrimination Committee), and Alexander Haig, *Caveat: Realism, Reagan*, 189.

32. *New York Times*, November 30, 1983, p. A8.

33. List from Satloff, ed., *Strategy and Defense*, 121–124, and from interviews.

34. Totals as given in interview with a DoD official who requested anonymity, February 1988.

35. Congressional Research Service, Memorandum of March 8, 1988, "U.S. Laws That Benefit Israel," 10.

36. See Robert S. Greenberger, "Israel Seeks to Obtain the Kind of Financial Aid That NATO Members Get from U.S. Government," *Wall Street Journal*, February 3, 1987, p. 70; and Hirsh Goodman, "Rabin in U.S. to Sign Agreement," *Jerusalem Post Weekly*, December 19, 1987, p. 4.

37. Rozenman, *United States–Israel Strategic Cooperation*, 12.

38. U.S. Department of State, Bureau of Public Affairs, "Working for Peace and Freedom" (Address by Secretary George P. Shultz, May 17, 1987), *State Department Current Policy*, no. 957, p. 3.

39. See Martha Wenger, "The Money Tree: U.S. Aid to Is-

rael," *Middle East Report* (Washington, D.C.), nos. 164–165 (May–August 1990): 13.

40. In April 1987, one experienced Washington reporter judged – in notable contrast to the judgment Shultz would deliver the following month – that "March may have been the cruelest month ever in U.S.-Israeli relations." Christopher Madison, "Tensions with Israel," *National Journal* 19 (April 4, 1987), 815.

41. Rozenman, *United States–Israeli Strategic Cooperation*, 11–12.

42. Dore Gold, "Strategic Ties with the U.S. Go on Regardless," *JPIE*, April 16, 1988, p. 8.

43. Text of coalition agreement as circulated in letter from David Peleg, minister of information, Embassy of Israel, Washington, D.C., December 23, 1988. For a description of the agreement, see *New York Times*, December 20, 1988.

44. For a good description of these disagreements, written in October 1989, see Jackson Diehl, "U.S., Israeli Right Differ on Peace Strategy," *Washington Post*, October 30, 1989, pp. A1, A21.

45. Washington Institute for Near East Policy, *U.S. Policy and the Middle East Peace Process: Fourth Annual Policy Conference*, Washington, D.C., 1990, 6, 7.

46. Nahum Goldmann, "Israel, the US, and American Jewry – A Complex Relationship," *New Outlook* 22 (October 27–30, 1979): 20. Goldmann had also been the founder and first chairman of the Conference of Presidents of Major American Jewish Organizations.

47. Blitzer, *Between Washington and Jerusalem*, 72–73.

48. Morris J. Amitay, "A Field Day for Jewish PACs," *Congress Monthly* (New York) 50, no. 4 (June 1983): 11.

49. Thomas Dine declined to be interviewed for this project, March 10, 1988.

50. See two pamphlets in the series *AIPAC Papers on U.S.-Israel Relations* (Washington, D.C.): Steven J. Rosen, "The Strategic Value of Israel," 1982, p. 11; and W. Seth Carus, "Israel and the U.S. Navy," 1983, p. 10.

51. Richard B. Straus, "Israel's New Super-Lobby in Washington: Reagan and Co.," *Washington Post*, April 27, 1986, Outlook section, C1–2.

52. Author interview with Ariel Sharon, July 1987.

53. Satloff, ed., *Strategy and Defense*, 82.

54. Steven L. Spiegel, "U.S. Relations with Israel: The Mili-

tary Benefits," *Orbis* 30, no. 3 (Fall 1986): 476. Other less comprhensive presentations of this case can be found in the AIPAC papers mentioned above, in many of the mid-1980s publications of the Washington Institute for Near East Policy, and in some of the contributions to edited works such as *The Soviet-American Competition in the Middle East*, Steven L. Spiegel, Mark A. Heller, and Jacob Goldberg, eds. (Lexington, Mass.: Lexington Books, 1988), and *Superpower Involvement in the Middle East*, Paul Marantz and Blema S. Steinberg, eds. (Boulder, Colo.: Westview Press, 1985).

55. This argument was adduced in an interview with a former State Department official friendly to Israel, March 1988.

56. Spiegel, "U.S. Relations with Israel," 476.

57. See Andy Court, "Spy Chiefs Gather to Honor Israel's Friend in CIA," *Jerusalem Post*, November 27, 1987, p. 1.

58. It has been argued that, while Sharon's portrayal of the risks and opportunities in Lebanon was unrealistic, that provided by Israeli intelligence chiefs at the time was more accurate. This does not, however, reduce the risks to the United States of relying on Israeli intelligence, because any such exchange would presumably always be kept under the control of the Israeli political echelon. It should be noted that 1982 was not the first occasion that Israeli intelligence (or the way it was processed at the political level) had failed miserably. In 1973 Israel's military intelligence organization failed to use available information to predict the Arabs' surprise offensive. See Schiff, *A History of the Israeli Army*, 194–203.

59. Author interview with Andrew Marshall, February 1988.

60. Interviews with Defense Department officials who asked not to be identified, February 1988 and December 1989. The last of these officials judged that "of all the U.S. relationships around the world, this is the one most driven by domestic politics."

61. Spiegel, "U.S. Relations with Israel," 480.

62. For details of these lessons, see Cobban, "Air-Defense Lessons of the Lebanese War," 257–270. Spiegel's version of what happened in the air-defense battle showed the hyperbole typical of the pro-Israeli "strategic salesmen." He claimed that "Israel proved that there was a means of breaking the antiaircraft missile wall that the Soviets thought they had developed against Western air forces." Spiegel, "U.S. Relations with Israel," 488–489.

63. Author interview with a DoD official who requested anonymity, March 1988.

64. Author interviews, February and March 1988.

65. Spiegel, "U.S. Relations with Israel," 481.

66. Author interview with Dov Zakheim, March 1988. He revealed, for example, that whereas the DoD had assigned 30 cost-scrutineers to the Lavi study, the Israeli Ministry of Defense had assigned only two. Another Pentagon analyst noted in an interview that the Israeli defense industry would also have to improve its quality assurance procedures if it wanted to meet DoD standards.

67. Cost estimate from Clyde R. Mark, *Israel: Foreign Assistance Facts*, Issue Brief, no. IB85066 (Washington, D.C.: Congressional Research Service, update of May 27, 1988), 6.

68. Spiegel, "U.S. Relations with Israel," 483.

69. This issue has been widely discussed in the Soviet media since 1985, with such senior Soviet commentators and analysts as Igor Belyayev and Yevgeniy Primakov warning about the inherent unpredictability Israel's possession of nuclear weapons has introduced into the global balance of nuclear terror. See Igor Belyayev, "A Bomb in the Cellar," *Literaturnaya Gazeta* (Moscow), October 23, 1985, p. 14, and October 30, 1985, p. 15, as translated in Joint Publications Research Service–Soviet Union International Affairs (hereafter JPRS-UIA) 86-006, p. 94; Yevgeniy Primakov's presentation at The Brookings Institution, Washington, D.C., December 1987; and Helena Cobban, "Soviet Views of Israel as an American Ally and a Nuclear Power," *Military Dimensions of Soviet Middle East Policy*, Helena Cobban, ed. (College Park, Md.: Center for International Security Studies at Maryland, 1988).

70. Spiegel, "U.S. Relations with Israel," 489, 492.

71. Author interview with an analyst who requested anonymity, February 1988.

72. Author interviews with analysts and officials who requested anonymity, February and March 1988.

73. These authors wrote that "the Saar V was considered by all branches of the [Israeli] planning staff (other than the navy) to be a potential floating Lavi." Goodman and Carus, *The Future Battlefield and the Arab-Israeli Conflict*, 60.

74. Veteran military assistance analyst Harry Shaw has written that "Israelis are . . . consistently hesitant to spell out the circumstances under which Israel would be willing to risk fighting Soviet forces when it has a choice in the matter." See

Harry J. Shaw, "Strategic Dissensus," *Foreign Policy*, no. 61 (Winter 1985–1986): 131.

75. Author interview with an analyst who requested anonymity, February 1988. This same effect of congressional earmarking has also been noted with respect to civilian economic assistance. The list of countries for which Congress earmarks FMS funds includes Israel, Egypt, the Philippines, Pakistan, and Morocco.

76. Author interview with Andrew Marshall, February 1988.

77. Author interview with an analyst who requested anonymity, March 1988.

78. Meron, "An Israeli Perspective on Strategic Cooperation," 107, 109.

79. Author interview with a DoD official who requested anonymity, March 1988. Richard Straus has noted that "pro-Israel sentiment on Capitol Hill seems to have taken on a life of its own, independent of the wishes of AIPAC or Israel itself." Straus, "Israel's New Super-Lobby."

80. Author interview with Richard Armitage, spring 1988.

81. Author interview with Ariel Sharon, July 1987.

82. Gabriel Sheffer, *Dynamics of Dependence: U.S.-Israeli Relations* (Boulder, Colo.: Westview, 1987), 3.

83. Author interview with Aharon Yariv, Tel Aviv, April 1988.

84. Ze'ev Schiff, "U.S. and Israel: Friendship under Strain," *The National Interest*, no. 10 (Winter 1987–1988): 7. In a prescient addendum to this observation, Schiff noted that Israel's policies in the occupied territories were "likely to result [in] riots, civil war, a major new war, or Israel's loss of its democratic character."

85. Author interview with Shai Feldman, February 1988. Dov Zakheim referred to this latter concern when he noted that "the opium of military assistance prevents tough budget management, resource allocation and weapons system development." See Dov Zakheim, "The Reagan Years: An American Net Assessment," *Between Two Administrations: An American-Israeli Dialogue* (Washington, D.C.: Washington Institute for Near East Policy, 1989), 18.

86. Shlomo Ma'oz, "U.S. Aid as Liability," *Jerusalem Post*, October 17, 1986, p. 20, as reproduced in FBIS-MEA-86-202, October 20, 1986, p. I8.

87. Author interview with Shai Feldman, February 1988.

88. Zakheim, "Yet the Lavi Lingers On and On. . . ."

89. In March 1988 Congress finally showed that its permissiveness toward Israel was not limitless. Thirty senators signed a letter to Secretary of State Shultz expressing open "dismay" that Israeli Premier Shamir was refusing to agree to any territorial compromise in the West Bank and Gaza. "Letter from 30 Senators to Shultz on Mideast," *New York Times*, March 7, 1988, p. 6.

90. For details, see Quandt, *Camp David: Peacemaking and Politics*, 103-104.

91. This lesson has relevance for the debate over whether the United States can effect the same leverage over Israeli decision making on the Palestinian issue. For some parts of this debate, see Helena Cobban, "If Arafat Utters the I-Word, Should Israel Say the S-Word?" and Joseph Alpher, "Why Israel Won't Promise a Palestinian Sovereignty: A Reply," *Moment*, Washington, D.C. (August 1989): 12-21.

92. Amir Oren, "The Next Phase of U.S.-Israeli Strategic Cooperation," *Policy Forum Report* 1, no. 8 (December 1989): 2.

93. Ze'ev Schiff, "Strategic Cooperation – Against Whom?" *Ha'aretz*, November 9, 1989, p. 13, as translated in FBIS-NES-89-219, November 15, 1989, p. 27.

94. In March 1990, George Shultz published an article in which he warned that "the Israelis, who have displayed discomfort at the idea of American support founded on moral commitment, preferring strategic cooperation grounded in the adversarial relationship of the superpowers, must reassess the changing global strategic environment. . . . The old idea of launching regional conflict to attract outside attention and gain leverage for your aims is no longer a viable approach – if it ever was." George Shultz, "Mideast Diplomacy in a Changing World," *Jerusalem Post*, March 9, 1990, p. 10; also published a few days earlier in the *Washington Post*.

Chapter 4

1. See, for example, Daniel Pipes, "Syria: The Cuba of the Middle East?" *Commentary* 82, no. 1 (July 1986): 15-22.

2. Efraim Karsh, *The Soviet Union and Syria: The Asad Years* (London: and New York: Routledge, 1988), 96.

3. Ibid., 97.

4. Hannah, *At Arms Length*, 47.

5. Comments from a Soviet Middle East analyst, November 1989.

6. For details of these years, see Karsh, *The Soviet Union and Syria*, 8–14.

7. For the text of the communiqué, see Quandt, *Camp David: Peacemaking and Politics*, Appendix 2.

8. For a thorough analysis of this issue, see V. A. Kremenyuk, "The United States in Regional Conflicts," *SShA:EPI* (Moscow), no. 6 (June 1986): 23–33; as translated in JPRS-USA-86-009, pp. 25–37.

9. A copy of the full public text of the treaty appears in Karsh, *The Soviet Union and Syria*, 122–125. It was also published in *Current Digest of the Soviet Press* (Columbus, Ohio) 32, no. 41 (November 12, 1980), 6.

10. Karsh, *The Soviet Union and Syria*, 55.

11. See Itamar Rabinovitch, *The War for Lebanon, 1970–1983* (Ithaca, N.Y.: Cornell University Press, 1984), 119.

12. "Soviet Ambassador Comments on Lebanese Situation," on Beirut domestic radio in Arabic, May 16, 1981; as translated in FBIS-MEA-81-095, p. G1.

13. Karsh, *The Soviet Union and Syria*, 59.

14. The Palestinians have pointed out that during the 1980s their communities in Lebanon came under repeated attack from both Syrian and Israeli forces. The major direct evidence Palestinians cite for the existence of some form of collusion in June 1982 was the simultaneous presence in Washington, for a short period, of both Israeli Defense Minister Sharon and President Asad's brother Rif'at al-Asad.

15. Author interview with Gennady Terasov, Moscow, July 1988.

16. Conversation with a Soviet expert who requested anonymity, November 1989.

17. For details, see Helena Cobban, "The Palestinians from the Hussein-Arafat Agreement to the Intifada," *The Middle East from the Iran-Contra Affair to the Intifada*, Robert O. Freedman, ed. (Syracuse: Syracuse University Press, 1990).

18. Hannah, *At Arms Length*, 32. His figures are calculated in constant 1987 dollars.

19. Interview with Igor Belyayev, Moscow, July 1988.

20. Author interviews with officials and analysts in Moscow, July 1988.

21. Quoted in Caryle Murphy, "Syria Urged to Stress Defense," *Washington Post*, November 20, 1989, pp. A1, A28. "Reasonable defense sufficiency" was the principle according to which the Soviets had been trying to downsize their own military force structure since 1987.

22. "Official Views Arab-USSR, Arab-U.S. Relations," *Al-Watan* (Kuwait), January 7, 1990, p. 18; as translated in FBIS-SOV-90-006, January 9, 1990, p. 33.

23. Elizabeth Kridl Valkenier, "Revolutionary Change in the Third World: Recent Soviet Assessments," *World Politics* 38, no. 3 (April 1986): 415.

24. K. N. Brutents, *National Liberation Revolutions Today*, vol. 2 (Moscow: Progress Publishers, 1977), 126. A broad review of the Soviet debates over Third World issues is provided in Jerry F. Hough, *The Struggle for the Third World: Soviet Debates and American Options* (Washington, D.C.: Brookings Institution, 1986).

25. Brutents, *National Liberation Revolutions Today*, 108, as checked and found to match the Russian text in K. N. Brutents, *Sovremennye natsional'no-osvoboditel'nye revolutsii* (Moscow: Politizdat, 1974).

26. Brutents, *The Newly-Free Countries in the Seventies* (Moscow: Progress Publishers, 1983), 147.

27. In early 1990 it remained unclear what effect the apparent downgrading of the CPSU's role in foreign affairs would have on Brutents's role.

28. Author interview, Moscow, July 1987.

29. Primakov, talk at the Brookings Institution, Washington, D.C., November 1987.

30. "Shevardnadze Speaks on Foreign Policy," *Pravda*, July 26, 1988, p. 4; as translated in FBIS-SOV, July 26, 1988, p. 30.

31. For further development of this analysis, see Michael MccGwire, *Military Objectives in Soviet Foreign Policy* (Washington, D.C.: Brookings Institution, 1987), 215.

32. Ibid., 215–216.

33. Y. M. Primakov, *Anatomy of the Middle East Conflict* (Moscow: Nauka, 1979; Russian-language edition, Mysl', 1978), 150, 151.

34. Ibid., 154–155.

35. Ibid., 310.

36. Y. M. Primakov, *Istoriya odnogo sgovora* (History of a deal) (Moscow: Politizdat, 1985), 314.

37. E [Y.]. M. Primakov, "Soviet Policy toward the Arab-Israeli Conflict," *The Middle East since Camp David*, William B. Quandt, ed. (Washington: Brookings Institution, 1988), 387.

38. Ibid., 409.

39. Author interview with Gennady Terasov, Moscow, July 1988. At the time of the 1973 Middle East war, the Egyptians had reportedly owned a small number of Soviet-made FROG missiles, one of which was fired into Sinai in the last days of the war. But former Egyptian Information Minister Mohamed Heikal later said that these missiles had been kept under Soviet operational control throughout. Author interview with M. Heikal, Cairo, June 1987.

40. See the examples cited in appendix 1, "Recent Soviet Sources on U.S.-Israeli Strategic Relationship and Israeli Nuclearization," in Cobban, *Military Dimensions of Soviet Middle East Policy*, 49–52. In 1985, Soviet commentaries still all referred to Israel's nuclear program as being a subset of the American program.

41. V. Kuznetsov, "Some Missiles for Scrap. But Others?" *Pravda*, December 19, 1989, p. 4; as translated in FBIS-SOV-89-243, December 20, 1989, p. 1.

42. Ibid.

43. Ibid., 2.

44. For some of the Soviet lessons learned in 1982, see Cobban, "Air-Defense Lessons of the Lebanese War," 257–270.

45. Author interview with Colonel-General Dmitri Volkogonov, Moscow, July 1988.

46. See Michael MccGwire, ed., *Soviet Naval Developments: Capability and Context* (New York: Praeger, 1973), 354.

47. See Efraim Karsh, *The Cautious Bear: Soviet Military Engagement in Middle East Wars in the Post-1967 Era* (Jerusalem: Jerusalem Post, and Boulder, Colo.: Westview, 1985).

48. See Seale, *Asad of Syria*, 398, and Francis Fukuyama, *Moscow's Post-Brezhnev Reassessment of the Third World* (Santa Monica, Calif.: RAND, 1986), 67.

49. Author interviews, Moscow, July 1988.

50. Francis Fukuyama, *Moscow's Post-Brezhnev Reassessment*, 67.

51. Melvin Goodman, in Cobban, *Military Dimensions of Soviet Middle East Policy*, 45.

52. Author interview with Viktor Kremenyuk, Moscow, July 1988.

53. Author interview with Colonel-General Dmitri Volkogonov, Moscow, July 1988.

54. Ibid.

55. See TASS report, "Egyptian-Syrian Ties," as published in FBIS-SOV-90-001, January 2, 1990, p. 4.

56. See Cobban, "The Palestinians from the Hussein-Arafat Agreement to the Intifada."

57. These included Georgiy Mirskiy of the Institute of the World Economy and International Relations and Sergei Rogov of the USA and Canada Institute, both interviewed in July 1988.

58. Interview with Georgiy Mirskiy, Moscow, July 1988.

59. Author interview with Karen Brutents, Moscow, July 1988.

Chapter 5

1. Some reports have been published indicating that, during the 1973 war, Soviet nuclear materials had been detected moving through the straits linking the Black Sea and the Mediterranean. The evidence on which such reports were based, however, was later deemed by U.S. nuclear specialists to have been inconclusive because the American sensors involved had subsequently been proven faulty.

2. In 1980 the European Community powers made a last attempt, through issuing their Venice Declaration, to play a helpful role in the Arab-Israeli peace process. But the United States signaled that it did not welcome such efforts.

3. See George, *Managing U.S.-Soviet Rivalry*, 382.

4. One comparison that might be made, for example, would be between the U.S. response to Israel's 1982 invasion of Lebanon and its response if the British government had reacted to IRA military activities by massively invading Ireland and besieging Dublin.

5. In December 1989 Republican senior statesman Senator Robert Dole proposed that a portion of the U.S. economic aid formally earmarked for Israel – as for other countries – might be

diverted to the emerging democracies of Eastern Europe. Although Dole did not pursue the proposal, the fact that such a seasoned politician felt confident about making it at all indicated some erosion of the previous political taboo on voicing such ideas.

6. The strong challenge that Iraq seemed to be launching in spring 1990 to President Asad's long-standing claims that the Syrian military was the "defender of the Arab nation" no doubt gave Asad continuing pause for thought.

Index

tion capabilities and, 16; strategic deterrence and, 16, 33, 71,
119, 143–46; superpower role in,
76–77; superpowers and, 76–77,
146–47; U.S. and, 108–9

Terasov, Gennady, 117, 127
Terrorist threat, 19, 28–29, 74, 81
Third World conflicts, diplomatic
progress in, 2. *See also* Regional
conflicts

United Nations Disengagement
Observer Force, 16–17
United Nations Security Council
Resolution 242, 14–15, 91
United States: Arab arms sales
and, 103; Arab-Israeli peacemaking and, 140–41; Egyptian aid
from, 22, 101, 140; Falangist
Party and, 44–45; Gemayel and,
47; Israel's border with Syria
and, 15–16; Israel's 1982 invasion of Lebanon and, 38, 40–42,
43–44; Jordanian relations, 31;
Middle East peace process and,
133–35, 140; sea lines of communication with Gulf, 100; Syrian
diplomatic contacts and, 13;
Syrian economic aid and, 114;
Syrian-Israeli conflict and, 108–
9
U.S.-Israeli relationship, 78–111;
Bush administration and, 92,
110–11; Congress's role, 105–6;
control of Israel's military actions and, 101–2; eastern Mediterranean and, 99–100; fighter
plane sales, 79; financial aid and,
26, 62, 63, 79–80, 88–90, 101;

Golan Heights and, 37, 85, 142;
intelligence cooperation and, 96–
97; Israel's battlefield experience
and, 97–98; joint military exercises and, 11, 84, 88; Joint Political-Military Group and, 61, 88,
110; military supplies and, 30,
64–65, 79, 100–101; moral aspect of, 78, 80, 92, 93–94; National Security Decision Directive 111 and, 87–88; 1981
Memorandum of Understanding
and, 11, 37, 82, 83–84, 102; 1987
Memorandum of Understanding
and, 89–90; 1988 Memorandum
of Understanding and, 91; pro-
Israel lobby and, 6; push and
pull factors, 92–95; Reagan administration and, 30, 33, 61, 81–
92, 106–10, 142; strategic cooperation and, 78–79, 90, 95–103;
strategic planning and, 80;
technology transfers and, 110;
U.S. policy-making and, 105–11,
141–42

Van Creveld, Martin, 60
Voice of America transmitters, in
Israel, 88
Volkogonov, Dmitri, 8, 129, 131–
32

al-Wazir, Khalil, 68
Weinberger, Caspar W., 82, 83

Ya'ari, Ehud, 30, 38, 85
Yariv, Aharon, 104

Zotov, Alexander, 120

DS
119.8
.S95
C63
1991

50610

327.569
COB
Pb

50610

Cobban, Helena

Superpowers and the Syrian-
Israeli Conflict

DATE DUE

DEMCO